in the
'*I*'

Easing Through Life-Storms

teZa Lord

In the *'I'*
Easing Through Life-Storms
By teZa Lord

Ocean Entertainment
www.tezalord.com
OceanEntertainmentBooks@gmail.com

First Edition October 2017 Transcendent Publishing
Second Edition March 2023 Transcendent Publishing

Cover art by teZa Lord
Illustrations by teZa Lord

ISBN- 979-8-9878728-5-7

Library of Congress Control Number: 2017915951

Printed in the United States of America

Praise for *In the 'I'*

"It's all about love, isn't it, this journey of ours? How to get love, how to live love, how to spread love. teZa Lord is one of those untiring foot soldiers of love without whom this life we live would be unbearable. This is the story of how some badass juvie girls, thanks to teZa, thanks to yoga, thanks to a badass hurricane, found refuge from the storm of life into the shelter of love."

Yann Martel, author of multiple award-winning, *Life of Pi*

"*In the 'I'* is a true-life spiritual adventure story, packed with suspense and helpful hints on how to breathe, be still and learn to love oneself. The actual storm that Lord describes is a metaphor for the human condition; her work with hard-core juvenile delinquent girls, an inspiration to those who wish to make a difference in today's world. This book is a must-read for anyone on a spiritual path."

Reverend Alma Daniel, author of the classic, *Ask Your Angels*

"teZa Lord is an angel of the heart, a sky dancer and dakini who has devoted her life to love, aesthetic beauty, and the art of transformation. In everything she does, every word she writes, every canvas she adorns, she points the way to light and a higher realm of being."

Wade Davis, author of many bestsellers, a favorite TED speaker, National Geographic Explorer, anthropologist, ecologist, recipient of the 2017 Award for Social Awareness from U. of British Columbia

"teZa Lord is a clear and conscious voice well worth your time and attention. Not only is she a fabulous writer/artist, but she is a true force for awakening."

Paul Samuel Dolman, author of bestseller *Hitchhiking With Larry David;* host: *What Matters Most* podcast

"A well told, deeply moving story of hope and redemption that will inspire you in your awakening. This book is a gem that you will want to read slowly and savor every passage!"

Dr. Steven Farmer, author of bestsellers *Sacred Ceremony*
and *Healing Ancestral Karma*

"Two Thumbs Up! I loved this book! Shows how we can all find peace, even in a noisy jail, even in the middle of a hurricane. An exciting book with an important message. I predict this book will become a classic."

Alan Garner, author of multiple bestsellers

"Wow! I really love this book! As a skeptical atheist with a cynical side, Lord's message of positivity and unconditional love, inspires and soothes the soul. Thank you teZa, for sharing your experience and message."

Patty Wagstaff, Aerobatic Champion, Airshow Pilot, Author,
Entrepreneur, Instructor

"teZa Lord narrates her story of bringing yoga to Florida's incarcerated teenage girls in present tense, reminding us all to stay present and open to inner wisdom."

Wah!, kirtan artist, yoga adept, and author of
Healing: A Vibrational Exchange

"I couldn't put it down! There's magic in the way teZa creates tension and fascination in the context of locked-up teen girls, meditation, yoga, and an imminent hurricane."

Rita Golden Gelman, author of *Tales of a Female Nomad: Living at
Large in the World*

"Throughout *In the 'I'* teZa Lord paints broad strokes, literally and metaphorically, not only telling it like it was, but opening doors for us to ponder ways that we know this story in our own lives."

Caren Goldman, author, *Healing Words for the Body, Mind and Spirit* and *Restoring Life's Missing Pieces*

"Author Lord has written a most wonderful, heartfelt account of redemption through love and yoga, under the shadow of Hurricane Charley. Her experience helps restore one's faith in humanity. Bravo, teZa!"

Jonathan Meader, artist, and author of *Ancient Egyptian Symbols* and *In Praise of Women*

"teZa Lord's new book is a transformative piece that works on so many levels you are bound to find a comfortable way in, and once ensconced there, a satisfying journey of spirituality. In the 'I' is the present moment we all should strive for, and *In the 'I'* is just the book to take us there."

John Miglis, novelist and screenwriter

"In a world besieged by natural and manmade catastrophes, Lord's message is timely and powerful. *In the 'I'* is a book that provides encouragement, peace, and a vision of good things in the lives of individuals, institutions, and the world, regardless of circumstances."

Nancy Quatrano, author and publishing consultant

"This book contains a most powerful message. By doing these practices we will become One with each other and with the Universe that surrounds all of us. *In the 'I'* is a must-read for everyone."

Eve Stoklosa, award-winning educator and consultant

"In the 'I' puts us in the center of a hurricane as we observe first-hand how the lives of these juvie girls are transformed both physically and spiritually. teZa Lord does an excellent job of capturing this real-life tempest, with exciting plot twists and quirky characters that spring off the page."

J. G. Sandom, author and internet entrepreneur

"This remarkable book is for any person who would welcome an inner quiet in what can be a noisy, anxiety-inducing world, work place, community or domicile—for even a yoga skeptic like myself!"

Robert D. Storey, corporate attorney and former Marine

"I loved *In the 'I'* and couldn't stop reading! It clearly demonstrates that our experiences, one by one, show us the way to freedom and how to shift our reaction to circumstances, no matter what, even when the storms of life hit. Thank you teZa Lord!"

Dr. Jami Martin, Life Changes and Transitions Facilitator

"As I read *In the 'I'* I found myself sobbing with overwhelming joy! I connect so deeply with the author's passion ... it felt like a ball of light beaming out of my chest from my soul as I read her beautiful words. My tears acknowledged how blessed I am that in my life, I too am gifted with this same connection teZa Lord conveys. And knowing there are so many other beautiful souls that feel and think the way we do makes my heart burst with joy at how contagious love is. As a teacher myself, I am so incredibly blessed that I get to bring Yoga, breathing and meditation to people. teZa has put into words what is in my heart ... So Much Love!"

Eva Marie Lowry, yoga teacher and retreat leader

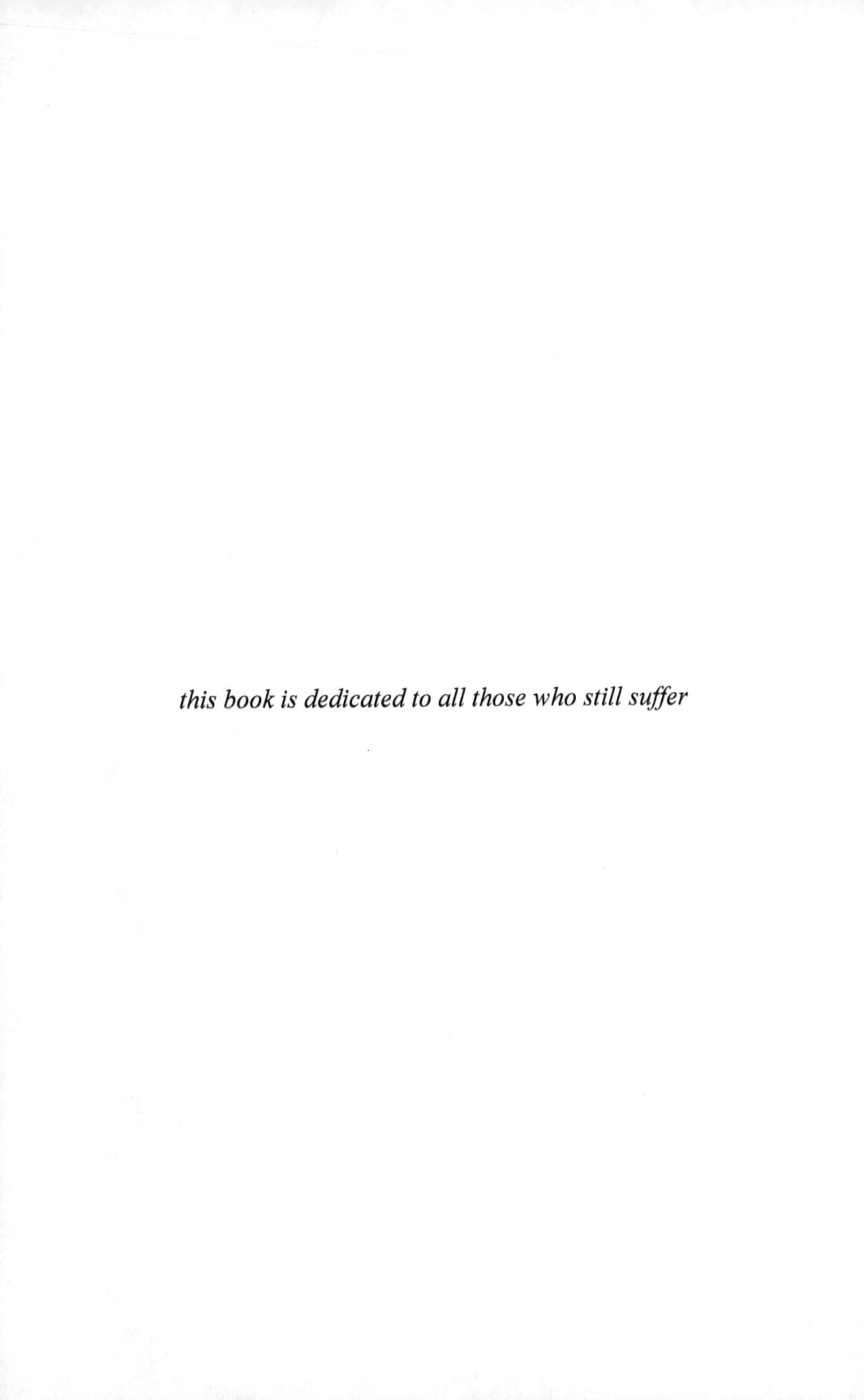

this book is dedicated to all those who still suffer

contents

introduction

Since this story took place, BIG changes have occurred in society. All around the world, yoga and cell phones are now ubiquitous, both of which were just gaining popularity at the time of these events. Three years before the particular hurricane season featured here, the uncertainty resulting from 9/11 became a commonly felt emotion worldwide. Politics has done nothing to assuage people's fears regarding terrorism. And now, with the dawn of a new White House upon us in America, things have become even more challenging. In today's world people have more fears and anxieties than they had a decade ago.

In the following true story, I draw a parallel between a person's own inner fear and the story of the fierce hurricane named Charley, when it struck an isolated prison filled with locked-up juvenile girls in 2004. Their story mirrors all of our stories. If you are filled with trepidation and fears about the world situation, you are locked up in your own self-made, internal prison. This is the story of how I used ancient techniques, in addition to love and compassion, to teach these distressed, angry girls the peace-instilling journey that can happen inwardly. These hardcore juvie delinquents had little joy in their high-security lockup in central Florida—before I volunteered to teach them yoga poses and other mind-stilling techniques. I hope what we went through together, many yesterdays ago, helps to alleviate some of the myriad causes of humankind's unease today. If my yoga girls could find inner peace—anyone can.

teZa Lord
St. Augustine, 2017

invocation

L et this true story be my offering for empowering those whose lives are not yet centered on their own truth within. By sharing these experiences, I hope to instill courage where once there was mistrust, disappointment, or anger: all masks of fear. Let this parallel universe of real events wash your soul with joyous surrender wherever there might be (even a little) self-imprisonment. Because it's true: you cannot live in harmony with *All That Is* if you insist on controlling others, or let others control your treasured inner state. Breathe deeply. Let us journey together. The inside adventure is simply—the Best!

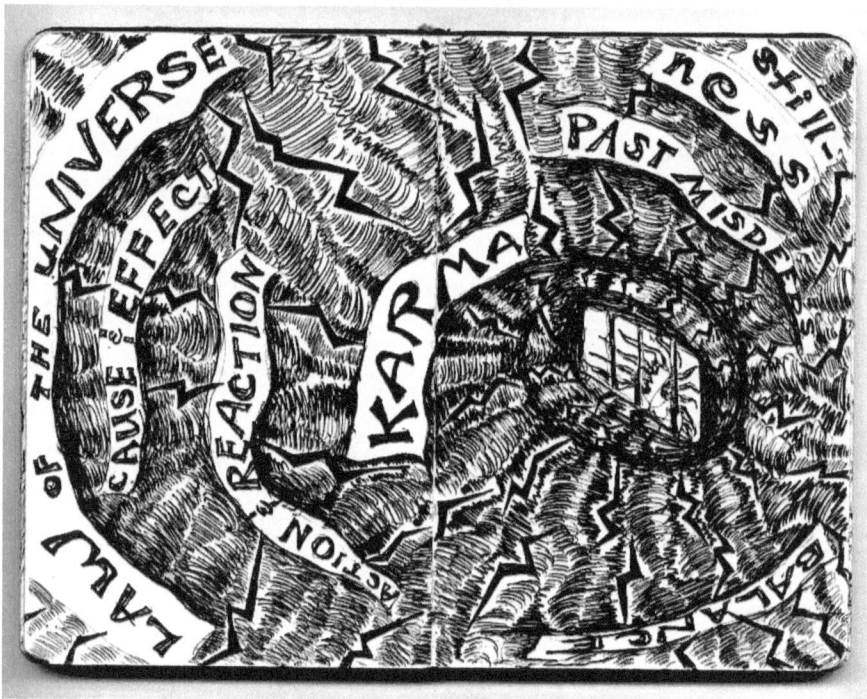

… deep in your heart … you know

CHAPTER 1

the teacher within

"Being in jail," I tell my girls as we stand to begin our sun salutes, "is unacceptable to you, I know. I've been there myself. But you yoga girls, you're beginning to see that even what appears to be the worst thing you would ever choose for your life, may just be exactly what your life needs."

I see their brows furrow, their eyes flashing, "Wha'...??"

"It's true," I say. "You're here. You know deep in your heart that you deserve to be here. You are responsible for everything that got you into this place, step-by-step, choice-by-choice. So—now that you're here, don't waste another moment being pissed about it." I take a deep breath and decide to go all the way in my explanation as I begin to stretch my body.

"Now that you're here, take a tally of your life and recognize that you can choose to benefit from this time in lockup, without the freedoms you're used to. Use these months, or years, in some cases ..."

I take another deep breath ...

"... and accept your being here, locked up for now, as a gift. A gift you don't want, but possibly one that may change your life. Clearly see that you got here due to your own choices, some of them pretty bad. Now, we can use this time together to still your mind, like we do with our breath, then the poses, and our final *savasana* meditation. Right this second you can make a decision to change your life—and you'll never be in prison again.

"Not behind bars, and never again on the *Outs* either, when you are physically freed from here. You don't ever have to feel imprisoned by anyone or anything, in your own life situation. You can choose, right here and right now, and remind yourself whenever you feel low, or like a victim, or want to blame someone else for your funk, depression or rage—that you can make your life a prayer."

"What d'you mean by that, Miss?" one of the girls barks.

"I mean that each moment of life is precious. And every choice you make adds up. You may not notice how things accumulate, but they do. The people you hang with, the thoughts you think, how you spend your time, even the food you eat. Every single thing adds up. Whatever choice you make results in you enjoying your life, or you hating your life—or worse, not caring either way.

"It's up to each of us to decide how our life is going to be. No jail, no government, and certainly not your *poor-old-me* thinking— nothing!—can make your life happy if you don't make it happy yourself."

The girls are quiet as we all stand, our breaths stilled, their minds chewing on what I just said. I take a deep breath, and they mimic me as I lift my arms up to our imaginary *sky* where I've taught my girls to envision an imaginary *sun* above us, inside the lockup walls. As we move, I speak.

"How powerful to know that our life—*let's bend our knees and bring our head and arms down toward the floor*—is our own to design—*now grab your ankles and pull hard*—each of us, ours to create just as we want."

We hang bent over, in rag doll, letting our bodies release all the tension our spines carry when they support us all day, every day.

As we relax from our waists, with everyone in class accustomed to this technique of unwinding our spines for a few breaths, I continue.

"Life is about just showing up. Our job, as awakened, aware persons—is to dance, and laugh, and enjoy the ride. Lighten up! Let go of control. Let spirit flow in your veins. Let the giggling goddess and god within lead this dance we do with the light of Being."

Audibly I take in air.

"Let's breathe in and, with tight abs, bring ourselves up to stand in mountain pose. Nice. That's good."

The girls and I stand taking in deep, noisy ocean-sounding breaths, just as I've taught them. After this little warm-up, and before we begin our official *surya namaskars*, I speak to my twelve yoga students, silent and open-hearted, with me in a big circle. I know how eager they are to change their up-till-now miserable lives.

"Today you're choosing the path of awareness by practicing yoga with me," I say as we stand in the stillness of mountain pose. "Awareness and nothing else, I guarantee you, makes us happy. I know this because I was just like you. And when I learned to give up all my old bad, negative addictions for the new good, positive addiction of loving myself—awareness filled my life. Yoga taught me the way by letting my own body be *the teacher within*."

watch your inner life open like a blossom

CHAPTER 2

breathe

When life attacks, or in the case of what happened to the yoga girls, when Nature attacks—what can we do?

Two choices present themselves when catastrophes occur: 1) We can freak out, shout and cry, shake our fists, go comatose, freeze with fear; or 2) We can choose to go within to the calm center of our Being, and thereby not be affected by *any* exterior circumstance.

The highly stressed-out girls to whom I taught yoga and meditation chose number two when Hurricane Charley came bearing down upon them, a natural disaster of paramount proportions. What happened to them can be applied to any of us, as we face our own disasters.

The teenage inmates at the Academy of Bowling Green (ABG) who found their way to my weekly yoga class realized, if they kept coming back, that they could choose to cultivate this stillness that helps us get through all of life's storms. *Doing yoga doing time,* as they called it in class, demonstrates beyond any philosophy or scientific explanation, that each of us has the power within to change. When doing yoga, our physical bodies show us the benefits of learning how to focus, and we become mentally and spiritually balanced as a result. Within the focused body is the teacher we all possess. If we're not focused, we can't hold a pose: It's as simple as that.

First though, we learn to breathe. "Well, of course you know how to breathe," I say to my girls with a laugh. "What I mean is that many of you have been breathing without an active aware-ness."

I explain further as we start to breathe together. "*Deep breath in.* Breath is the key to everything. *Long breath out.* Breath stills us or excites us. *Deep breath in.* When we learn to watch our breath, *long breath out,* we become engaged with the process. *Deep breath in.* Conscious breathing stills the mind. *Long breath out.* Our minds become … *Breath in* … focused … *Breath out.* Focused on what? *Breath in.* Only on our breathing ….

"Let's continue in silence for a few breaths in and out."

After the girls start our session with simple breathing awareness exercises, we choose an asana. I demonstrate a tree pose. Then we do it together. With step-by-step instructions ("Continue to watch your breath as we align the body"), the girls see they can achieve this challenging balance pose. Shouts of joy spontaneously erupt.

"Look at me! I can do it!"

"I can't believe it! I'm standing on one leg, check it out!"

We laugh. We marvel. We're doing yoga on the *Ins*, in jail. Or for you, probably on the *Outs*.

Every one of my yoga girls (and now, you) discovers—from the very first moment of awareness— that they're totally in control of their breath, quickly followed by achieving an otherwise impossible, yet simple pose. And the takeaway from this is knowing we all have an innate power within.

The ancient practice of yoga is a science. In today's world it's been embraced as more than simply a form of exercise, like running, aerobics or weight lifting. The focus on breathing, and the inner stillness *watched breath* brings, begins the journey inward. Who cares about this breathing thing? Anyone who wishes to know the calm and joy and, ultimately, the serenity of a spiritual life. People do yoga to balance all aspects of their mental, physical and emotional selves.

For the inmates at ABG, the yoga we do in our weekly class gives them all the tools they need for personal empowerment. That's the magic word they've been hearing and desperately need, to stop wanting to either kill themselves or bust out of this godforsaken prison they're locked-up in.

Exactly what every stressed-out individual on planet Earth hopes for sooner or later. *Empowerment*. Spiritual calm.

The calm within our being—the *inner 'I'*—is each person's core of serenity.

Everything breathes, even the cosmos. Look at planets, supernovas, and galaxies as they swirl in and out, when seen through long-range radio telescopes. They surely appear as if they are breathing. From inside our own body, where we must breathe oxygen to refresh our billions of cells; to the farthest outreaches of space, where some presume we might one day find more than our known Universe: breath exists. Air. Space. In motion, breathing. But what substance is breathed away from our home planet? We don't know. Maybe stardust? Some say we on Earth breathe stardust in our atmosphere's O molecules. The only certainty in the realm of exploration, whether of cosmology or sociology, is that everything is connected … by the breath of consciousness. Without breath, at least here on Earth, there is no life.

A hurricane is when the breath of our world, planet Earth, becomes congested.

For someone who's stressed, breath is the link from their most basic survivor-self (to stay alive, we breathe) to another, less obvious, inner Being, which is called many things: the higher Self, Better-me, self-esteem, or plain ol' Inner Peace—the *'I'*. Our innate wisdom is our Salvation. We all have the ability to save our own selves. Relieving life's torments begins by connecting to the power of our breath.

This is why all good teachers of mind-body subjects focus on exercises that teach us awareness of ... breathing in ... breathing out.

Take a moment or two and do it here. Watch your Self breathe for a few rounds.

After all, if you're not breathing—you're dead. Now you're just checking: Yes, I'm very much alive. I'm even more aware of being alive now through this long breath in I'm taking ... and this long breath out I'm doing.

Yes, I'm alive. Yes, I'm present. Yes, I'm here, right now.

The news tells us what to expect tomorrow. Hurricane Charley's eye—around which the most ferocious part of this massive storm spirals—might reach us here at ABG, this itsy pinpoint on the map in the midst of rolling countryside. Anything might happen, tomorrow. The girls at yoga class today, Thursday August 12th, 2004, are uneasy, upset, and breathing in chest-heaving, hyperventilating freak-out mode. Every one of the dozen teenage girls present is sick with worry about their families. Every girl is from a different part of Florida. Every person who lives in Florida knows that a hurricane's path is completely unpredictable. Its deadly course can change in a heartbeat, meaning wind and flood disaster for one section of the state and a sunny calm day for another, just seventy miles distant from a storm's eye.

The storm's predicted path, the newscaster said, is for landfall sometime tonight after midnight, "Probably around the Tampa Bay region." This part of the coast is closer to where I live, in Lackland, than where ABG is located, in the central part of our peninsular Gulf of Mexico state. In yoga class, those girls whose families lived in Tampa and St. Petersburg, where strong and solid Ursula, the director of ABG, drives from every day, are the most stressed out.

Hurricane Charley is on its way, we all know. A direct hit is expected sometime tomorrow for the St. Pete/Clearwater/Tampa area. All of Pinellas, Manatee, and Hillsborough Counties are on ready alert. The girls' guards tell their charges the latest reports from their transistors, as they enter the big common room that doubles as our yoga room in our back-to-back classes. Girls whose families live in these coastal counties are beside themselves with worry. Prison is prison, though, even with bad weather. No phone calls except in an emergency allowed. When mandatory evacuation is enforced for the area, which won't happen until early the next day, the girls still won't have an opportunity to call their loved ones. Prison life is tough.

Here in today's class, I greet my yoga girls.

"I know you're all feeling super anxious today. We'll have a chance to share how we feel in our opening time. But first, let's begin with watching our breath."

The girls form the customary circle and sit quietly. The sound of my voice must comfort them, I think, because their lively chatter stops. They know that practicing yoga is a peaceful experience, even though we work hard at our poses.

"Let's close our eyes now. Watch your breath as you draw it slowly into your lungs … watch as it slowly leaves your nose, mouths closed. Just as we do at the beginning of each class, acknowledge that we're here, nowhere else. We're watching as we breathe in again, very slowly …."

Outside these thick concrete walls and iron-barred windows, the day seems steamy and quiet, as it always does in August. Every now and then a rogue gust of wind, mysteriously short and fierce, blasts against the shatterproof window panes. As the girls breathe, sets of eyes pop open to see the windows rattle from these mysterious *burps* of Charley's force that precede every hurricane, by a day at least. The girls glance nervously at the plastic bulletproof windows of the common room, where we hold our weekly class. We have no mats, no props, just an old Rasta box I bring to play soothing music. I use tapes because we are pre-digital, even pre-CD. My tapes are worn. I've used them for every yoga class I've taught for the two years I've been coming here. Girls come and go, depending on the length of their sentences. Today, everyone knows what's coming tomorrow. A killer-storm. The surprisingly fierce gusts, and their own increasing anxiety, are the only signs of the monster approaching us.

It's a Thursday like every Thursday when I arrive at Bowling Green with my music tapes and bag of terry facecloths to protect the girls' pretty chins and cheeks when we do a floor pose facedown. Like I said, we have no mats. The girls are in their stiff polyester uniforms, hoisting the suits up to free their limbs, to achieve our challenging positions. No fancy-pants spandex yoga duds here. No incense. No peaceful atmosphere either, especially when there's a takedown being done in the cafeteria or the hall, both adjacent to our spacious common room.

While driving to see my girls-in-lockup earlier today, I heard the news that Charley, now at Category 3, is due to hit Cuba late tonight. I'm uneasy, sure. But I've been through too many hurricanes to panic. I know what to do. My family back in Lackland is safe: we have extra water and food on hand, and everything's already boarded up from the last storm. I've done Reiki on my tall oaks, like I do when any strong storm heads our way.

Having lived and worked as an ex-pat in the Caribbean islands for a decade, I'm well acquainted with hurricanes and their deadly wrath. Here in Florida, smart storm preparation is a part of daily life during hurricane season. As the twelve girls who've signed up for yoga this week file in, with Mr. Lawrence as their sole guard, I see how the simple act of forming our opening circle instantly quells their chatty nerves. The rude pushing and shoving stops—as soon as they sit with me.

We begin each class with this group centering. We watch our breath. We chant a big, long *Ommm.* "To change the energy within us and inside this room," I say. I hand the carton containing the inspiration cards to the girl next to me, who selects one or two, not randomly as I'd prefer, before handing them to the next girl. Each small card I've made is inscribed with an attribute of awareness. I remind my girls, "Now we get to discuss life from a yogic perspective.

"It's time to shift gears with our thinking mind," I say. "We can change the way we feel, by changing how we think. How? First we'll watch our breath for a little while, to remember that our body is a powerful tool for focusing. Watching the breath helps to quiet our busy minds.

"After we identify the feelings your card brings up we can discuss them, then we'll do our asana practice. That's when we can use our body's ability to create, with steady focus, the poses today. Without our mind first steadied by breath-watching, the poses are impossible to do. When our mind is centered, only concentrating on a pose, there's no room in our consciousness for anything but stillness, peace, and calm. That's why our bodies—our own bodies!—can be, when properly trained, our best friend, and our best teacher."

I look around the circle. Everyone in attendance today, unlike other times, is a regular. There's no new girl to teach why breath is the path to shifting our awareness from lazy to hyper-alert. Or why we sing the ancient sound of *Om*, written about in the earliest of yoga's sacred scriptures, the Rig Veda, and later the Upanishads and the Yoga Sutras. I tell the girls anyway, "Remember that the word Om, classically pronounced *Aum,* is related to the Amen spoken by Christians, and Allah by Muslims. All things are connected by this holy sound."

I smile at seeing relief on the girls' faces after breathing and Om-ing.

"Today we need to lighten up. Not be paralyzed by fear."

Still, my yoga girls are restless. They murmur and shift where they sit, scared to the core by Charley's looming presence. Worried about their families, their babies. Six of these twelve girls before me have babies back home. None is over eighteen. The youngest is thirteen. They come to my class each week and claim to love what yoga does for them.

"We'll have fun today," I say, "even though a hard time might be upon us tomorrow."

I look around at the now-quiet circle. Everyone is listening. No one fidgets. I glance over at Mr. Lawrence, who's slouched in a soft chair off in the corner, his usual disinterested, aloof self. Held right up to his ear is his official walkie-talkie radio, crackling with the muffled sounds of activity he monitors from all sections of the sprawling facility.

"Who wants to share the word from their card today," I ask.

Lakeesha raises her hand, saying, "I got Self-discipline." Then Mimi shouts out, "I got Strength!"

I beam at them. "Those two words, more than any others, together mean Self-empowerment. Today, yes, all of us are strong! And wow, you guys in yoga class have learned to be self-disciplined, unlike most of your pals who don't come. By doing the breathing exercises and the poses, we're strengthening our inner selves. We can get through anything, can't we, with this kind of Self-control!"

The girls all laugh, dispelling the somber mood of minutes before. They share a few more attributes written on their cards to initiate dialogue that touches on deeper issues.

We talk briefly about Patience, Acceptance, Humor—each of the girls shares how she thinks the quality on her card applies to her.

"I'm not very patient," Lakeesha says. "But I'm trying, here in yoga class."

"I have a hard time accepting I'm not free," Katy says, "but yeah, I keep trying."

"I like to laugh a lot, sometimes too much!" giggles Marybeth.

I hear a throat-clear from the corner. Mr. Lawrence, the thirty-something, black prison guard, in his crisp white uniform shirt, is still lounging in his seat. Bearing his usual sour-grapes expression, he listens to the radio chatter. I know from past experience that he's a skeptical guy. Every time one of the girls turns to him after we've said, "Namaste" (*I see the light within you*), and repeats, "Namaste," to Mr. Lawrence, he replies mockingly, "You too, have *a nice day*."

He sees me looking at him and rolls his eyes as he sits sanctimoniously in his corner, separate from us. Some of the other guards will join us, sitting on the floor, breathing consciously, chanting an opening Om, choosing an attribute-card to talk about, trying to manage a steady pose. Some even try to meditate, with one eye on the girls and an ear to their turned-down but never mute walkie-talkies. But not this man. I think of him as the *Bad Guard,* while Estelle, the head of the twenty or so staff of male and female guards, is the *Good Guard*. Although these two are extremes on the scale, no one is as gruff and devoid of compassion as this dude, Lawrence. Thank goodness, I think, that Estelle is as sugary-nice as Lawrence is nasty wise guy. And Ursula, the director of ABG, well, I personally believe she's a real live angel who works for The System just to make it better.

Miss Estelle, the title mandatory for all adult females, whether married or single (so I'm always called *Miss* teZa), is kind, caring, and funny, and tries to achieve some semblance of yoga with us. She never disagrees with me, rolls her eyes or criticizes, while Mr. Lawrence's negative body language expresses disapproval even now, in front of my yoga girls. I sigh. It's hard enough teaching these so-called *bad* girls without having to deal with his confirmed *bad attitude*.

Why am I teaching yoga to those society has deemed *bad girls* in this isolated, no-frills high security lockup? Back home, where I live with my husband Will and stepson Jonny, Kara, my own sixteen-year-old stepdaughter, has turned her back on me. Will and I have raised her and Jonny since she was seven and he was four, but for the past couple years my heart has been broken by Kara's right-on-time, adolescent rejection of me. Healthy, all the authorities say, yet painful nonetheless.

Two years before, I decided to share my greatest passions, yoga and meditation, with teenage girls who might appreciate what I had to offer, since my own stepdaughter sure didn't. When Kara reached puberty, she bought into the hatred her bio-mom had loudly spewed for me since I married her dad, seven years before. So I turned to other sources to share my discoveries on how to experience the thrill of life. I was determined to find girls who'd appreciate me and what I had to offer, as opposed to my uninterested stepdaughter. That's how my desire to teach the girls at ABG began.

Today's circle might hear bits of this familiar story that are new to them. When Tiffany, now called Matrika in class (some girls choose yoga names only for use during our time together), draws the card *Honesty*, I ask them to expand on who they think their teacher really is.

"I'm just like you, as I always remind you," I start off. Their eyes open wide. Oh boy, more juice about the odd redheaded lady who comes each week! "That's right, girls. Only I didn't get caught as early as you, but I did end up later like you, in jail."

Now every girl sits up straight. There is no disinterest at hearing this pronouncement of mine. "Say whaa—?" the teen chorus exclaims. Some of those who've been coming for a while show a knowing smile. They've heard this before when I let loose some detail every once in a while. The longer-term residents have heard it all before. My She-pirate past is no secret in my yoga class.

"Yes, I was once called a bad girl like all of you. Words! Don't buy into those labels! I was abused as a child like most of you were, as we've discussed before. By my teenage years I was a full-blown alcoholic, to mask the pain. Drugs weren't available then like they are now. But later, I got into drugs, too. For the past twenty years I've been in recovery. Clean and sober and doing yoga like a crazy lady.

Yoga is my high. I love the empowering and meditative aspects. So remember—while you're here in lockup, go to those AA meetings! They'll teach you how to live without using, on the Outs—one day at a time."

I look around. The girls are entranced. No one comments, so I continue.

"When my stepdaughter started acting out, I realized I couldn't reach her anymore. We used to be best friends. Then suddenly, I was her worst enemy. I contacted Girl Scouts Headquarters and asked, 'How can I help disadvantaged, at-risk girls?' I didn't tell the lady I wanted to help girls who are like I was. I wasn't *really* bad but being called that only confused me. So of course I acted out twice as badly, to live up to that label, one my parents first gave me. Sound familiar?"

I look around the circle and see heads bobbing in unison.

"What I shared with the Girl Scouts lady was that I wanted to help 'the worst cases, girls no one else can handle.' Because no one helped me learn who I was, not at your age. That came much later, after I got into big-time trouble and ended up doing some jail time like you all are, but in a Third World rat-hole, worse, much worse, than ABG. After I got released I finally got sober. Otherwise I'd probably be dead. It wasn't till then, though, that I asked for help. If anyone tried to help me before I was ready to stop acting out, I wouldn't have listened."

"What did she say?" Shay asks.

"And how'd you find us?" Megan demands. "Nobody ever comes to teach us except hardcore Christian ladies."

I laugh. "Ah, my story hits home, eh? Well, the Girl Scouts lady suggested all sorts of ways to help teenage girls. I could teach one-time workshops to privileged, suburban lassies, for instance. But instead I chose to come here, to teach you guys."

"You did?" Tanondra says.

"You guys are perfect for me," I said. "I knew from my first time here that you really needed yoga, so … I kept coming. As soon as I met Miss Ursula she said, right after that big hug she gave me, 'I knew you'd come! I've been praying you up.' She'd been waiting, knowing I or someone like me would show up, she said. Because she knew you guys *really* needed the transformative power of yoga and meditation."

"Wow," L-Shezza says, speaking for everyone in our circle.

CHAPTER 3

home is where the big heart is

This place for youthful lawbreakers is not a pretty picture. Crowded together in a stark, bare bones correctional facility, guarded by mostly sullen men and women with noisy walkie-talkies, surrounded by an unbroken circumference of sinister-looking, privacy-black plastic-draped, razor-topped chain-link fences, these girls are disturbed, often violent and addicted to acting-out when they can't get their head-tripping drug of choice.

Some of the girls have exotic-ethnic names, Lakeesha, Mayendra, Eternia, Sha'Ron. One whom everyone calls Shay has such an extraordinary literary-inspired name that when I first met her I wanted to change my name to hers on the spot—ShakespearesDelight. It's her first name. I never knew anyone's last name, nor did I care. As a white woman I got to see firsthand that people of color prefer unique, complex names: L-Shezza, and Tanondra. Hardly any Marys or Janes in this group. Other girls, mostly whites and Hispanics, have typical American names: Melissa, Brittany, Tiffany, and way too many Jessicas.

Whatever the name, the possibility of any inmate, or *resident,* as Ursula calls her charges, being a normal teen, capable of having a typical messed-up adolescent life, is all but impossible. Many are already mothers. The majority have been battling addiction for years. Quite a few are HIV-positive, although that's kept confidential.

Despite such drawbacks as lack of funds for extras (meals are brought in by a caterer, cutting the cost of a kitchen and serving staff), those who teach the girls at ABG try their best to offer tools to make wiser choices, both now and when they're on the Outs.

I've lived through many hurricanes, yet I'm sensitive to others' fears at times like this. Anyone facing an oncoming threat has those questions of what if, what might, what, what, what? Anything can happen in a deadly storm like the one coming for us. It's a crap shoot. A hit or miss only God, or Nature, knows anything about.

As I drove the hour-long journey to the two sessions of yoga I teach each Thursday, the radio broadcasts Charley's predicted path has been altered again, by a few degrees. As it traveled toward Cuba—surprise, surprise—the storm changed course again, like hurricanes do. No matter how many degrees it bounced off track, by this time tomorrow we'd be seeing plenty of uprooted trees, disappeared roofs, dilapidated barns and outbuildings gone, and lots of flimsy houses destroyed, hit-or-miss.

As I drove I figured, even if, for some freaky reason, Charley's eye doesn't strike within a hundred-mile radius of us, by late Friday night or early Saturday, the landscape here will not be the same as it is on this peaceful and sunny Thursday morning.

Folks living along Florida's shores are preparing to scramble for cover. But those of us who live along the gulf coast and inland in the central region are feeling the most vulnerable. No one knows where Charley's path will go, once it crashes into the American continent. It hasn't even reached Cuba yet, but its speed is accelerating. Forecasters predict once it hits the large island mass and travels over that mountainous terrain, it might slow somewhat. But right after it leaves the island of Cuba, which won't be until much later tonight, perhaps in the early hours of Friday the 13th, the hurricane center says it will once again gather speed as it travels over the large expanse of the Gulf of Mexico before slamming into Florida's western coast.

Over open ocean is where a cyclonic storm gains strength and becomes an uber-killing force. Anything can make it change direction. I've seen hurricanes do 180-degree turns, unpredictable zigzags, even completely insane 360s for no apparent reason. Storms demonstrate the most dramatic of Nature's chaotic, schizophrenic character traits.

The day before a hurricane is predicted to hit, with so many variables ... there's no way to know what's going to happen; when or where. Or even if.

This Thursday, the day before Charley's predicted to hit us, apprehension runs thick like Jell-O in the veins of the citizens of Florida. It's hard to breathe. Shelves of grocery stores are bare; no bottled water, food, batteries are available—none of the necessities in a disaster. As I drove toward ABG I reminded myself to demonstrate inner calm to my yoga girls. For their sake.

Later, in class, I'll use the oncoming storm as an opportunity to share a basic yogic concept: the only peace in life possible is what we have inside. Our *inner 'I'*. After our opening circle we discuss what's on the girls' minds, and that's when I'll interject what I'm formulating on the drive over.

A lot of the girls have come to respect me as much as I love them. They trust me. They've grown to see how everything I share with them is true, even though I've always told them not to believe me. "Just because I say something's true, check it out for yourself," I always say. With every class I tell them, "Find out for yourself. Do yoga here with me, and watch your inner life blossom, like a flower. From fearful to trusting—your lives will transform beyond your wildest dreams."

I smile now. The girls in class today, they know. Before yoga, they didn't. And it all started with learning to watch their breath.

"Everyone here," I begin, "is experiencing the heart-stopping threat to our safety that's coming. We don't know whether we'll get a puff of Charley's outer rim or its most destructive part, its eye, dead-on. All we truly know is what our breath shows us—that we're alive. And today, everyone in this circle is facing the unknown."

I look around me. Everyone's listening. So I continue.

"I've been through several eyes of monstrous hurricanes. So let's talk a minute about that possibility tomorrow. It's a staggering reality that might happen."

"Really, Miss?" one of the girls squeaks.

"Yes, Maya, we have to be honest. It's better to be prepared for the worst than not, right?"

Everyone nods her head.

"This structure is super-strong. You have my word, I know buildings. Miss Ursula has had professionals tell her this building is the strongest around. So if the eye comes anywhere near, you can rest assured this building isn't going to blow away.

"Knowing you're safe inside these walls helps, right?" I add.

Heads nod again. I ask if anyone has a question. The circle remains quiet, so I continue.

"Preparations are in place. Mr. Eric the maintenance man has nailed shut anything loose, brought in anything untied, and is working hard to ready the generator, Miss Ursula told me."

"We love Mr. Eric," many of the girls chirp. "He's kind."

"He is. Kindness goes a long way, doesn't it? After ensuring our structure is safe, there's absolutely nothing one can do—when you're in the center of a cyclone—except to relax, and to keep breathing. That's after you've done everything to prepare for the storm beforehand. And we certainly have had enough time to do that. Mr. Eric has, everyone here at the academy has, and my own family and Miss Ursula's and Miss Estelle's have as well. Nature is not always kind, girls. Out West in places like Montana where I've visited, there's no time to prepare when deadly firestorms are driven by fierce and changing winds.

"When the actual moment hits, when a vicious Category 4 slams into your life, as Hurricane Charley is possibly about to do to us, here's what we can do, today: Touch the sturdy walls around you, acknowledge the beams and strong roof, the building you believe will never buckle from outside forces—and breathe as steadily as you can. Let's start praying today that all of us, and all those you love, survive this storm.

"Because that's all anyone can do, from the most capable to the least, from the smartest to the dumbest, from the prettiest to the homeliest, from the richest to poorest. Whether we're on the Outs or inside prison walls, when disaster strikes, believe with all your mind, soul, and body—you've done all you can.

"And keep breathing. Steadily, deeply, calmly. That's how we let go of fear. By concentrating on our breathing in, our breathing out."

A teacher ought to know ahead of time how best to help her students. In this case, mine are two classes of twelve each. There are fifty-two so-called "bad girls" imprisoned in this former factory built in the middle of nowhere. The cement block building that houses the girls was once a canning factory before its previous incarnation, a sprawling country and line-dancin' bar, preposterous for this land-locked region with the name, *Elmer's Off the Beach*. Before this iteration it was a grits 'n' eggs, cattle-and-citrus, truck stop restaurant.

Ursula joked with me soon after we met that she wished she could change the formal name, mandated by State authorities, from the Academy of Bowling Green to *Miss Ursula's Dream Home for Wayward Girls*.

"I manifested Estelle Smith to help me run this place, just like I did the building itself," Ursula said about the smiling and sturdy, gorgeous black lady who has worked as head guard at the academy since its earliest days. Ursula created every aspect of this experimental youth incarceration. From transforming the facility to accommodate psychological and wholeness healing, to choosing the benign sandy-color of its stucco walls, she's made this a large friendly home, complete with turquoise shutters to hide the reality of uniformed guards and un-shackled inmates. Passersby never notice the high security fences in the rear, with their coiled razor topping. Ursula's experimental facility was designed entirely by implementing ideas based on Alfred Adler's approach to helping better the human condition. When I asked Ursula what, exactly, that meant, she said, "To help each of our girls feel she *belongs* and is *significant*."

On August 10th Charley nearly arrived, as a gentler storm, a tropical depression, on Jamaica, that land of reggae beats; but it missed the island's westernmost edge. Gathering force, on August 11th its winds were clocked at a Category 1 hurricane. Then quickly, the storm was declared a Category 2 by the time it left the vicinity of the tiny Grand Cayman Islands, northwest of Jamaica, hundreds of miles south of Cuba. Once again traveling across open seas, Charley began to act really crazy, gathering speed and intensity. Hurricanes are known for their unpredictable nature, just like society's neurotics are. Every gigantic system of ferociously swirling wind becomes a slave to the concentric forces of Nature when over open water. Under these conditions a hurricane spins itself into a frenzy, intensifying its maze of interconnected cyclones whirling around a singular, tightly formed vortex—where, at dead center is its eerie, always-calm eye. A *cyclone* is the official name of a circular storm in the Pacific region; hurricane is used exclusively in the Atlantic region.

When a hurricane travels over land it slows, but over open ocean it quickly regains any speed it's lost while traversing terra firma. Which is exactly what happened to Charley when it hit Cuba, the first large land mass it ripped into as an official hurricane (except the tiny dots of the Caymans, and much earlier when a tropical depression,

Grenada and Barbados). Cuba was Charley's first obstruction since its birth as a tropical wave that formed on August 4th, five thousand miles away off the western coast of Africa.

Charley slammed into Cuba as a Category 3 hurricane exactly at midnight. Its maniacally insane salsa beat was the first to raise a toast on Fidel Castro's 78th birthday, on that inky-sky night at the start of Friday the 13th. Much later, scattered news accounts leaked to the rest of the world that twenty-one deaths would be attributed to Charley on the island, but bedridden *papa* (the people's favored nickname for *el lider* Fidel) survived, recovering from who-knew-what months after the storm struck.

Charley rammed Cuba in the large city of Batabanó, walloping the populace, traveling the longitudinal narrow width of the island in just two hours. There it struck Havana before exiting the island's northern coast. The storm's intensity knocked down or flooded everything in sight. At its core, the eye's winds were clocked at top speeds of 150 mph during its short land-jump over Cuba. After making a debacle of the stunned, devastated island, Charley would accelerate as soon as it left land, quickly reaching Category 4 deadly winds as it headed over open seas, straight for Florida's gulf coast.

Barreling through the skinniest part of the island, Charley howled and fitfully flung itself upon Cuba, taking its vengeance out on Fidel's people on his special day. Charley crashing Fidel's birthday party has people remembering *Carlos el terrible* to this day. They think of *Carlos el huracán* instead of their sick old leader, who, soon after his mysterious sickness struck, would retire and cloister himself from the public. But on the night Charley hit Cuba, *el papa* lay near death, according to clandestine reports in Miami. At two in the morning the angry tempest plowed through Havana.

Just as musicians and dancers gave up on making their wet way home and instead, partied all that night, Charley left the northwestern coast of Cuba between Playa Baracoa and Mariel. Its eye directly struck fifteen miles west from downtown Havana.

Slowing from its zany mambo dance over the island's fertile fields, Charley headed for open ocean. Here is where a hurricane gets out of hand, when leaving a huge land mass. For reasons no one has ever figured out, Charley bounced and bopped its vindictively cruel, erratic path arcing with each new course-change directly for Florida, as if a giant magnet were bringing it closer to land with each shift in its salsa dance. After leaving Cuba, Charley turned more northerly, then ever more easterly as it gathered energy. Just as it rammed through the festivities of Fidel's birthday, handing out flood and wind and death instead of party favors, Charley grew ever more wrathful as it moved toward the North American continent.

Stateside meteorologists told nervous listeners that its predicted course was changing again. The major city of Tampa and its environs of several million residents, including the surrounding suburbs where I lived in Lackland, wouldn't be the only area with people scurrying like scared rabbits as soon as they awakened.

On Thursday evening, before they went to bed, most residents on the entire Gulf of Mexico side of Florida had already endured long lines to fill their gas tanks. There wouldn't be any fuel left when they woke on Friday the 13th. Tampa, at the end of the long, curved dotted-line track superimposed on TV weather maps, was where forecasters predicted Charley's eye would strike continental America. That was if—the big *If*—the hurricane continued on the same projected path it assumed while traveling through Cuba.

Clearwater and St. Pete soon were jarred awake to the news that Charley had abruptly turned right, in an almost ninety-degree turn, as hurricanes are wont to do. The only good news was how slowly the massive storm traveled forward, now less than fifteen miles an hour. Sweeping over the smooth wide sea, the watery whirling dervish gathered force. When I went to bed the storm was headed straight for

Tampa—where I live only thirty miles inland. When I awake on Friday, Charley is now headed somewhere more south on the coast.

As soon as everyone is up they hear Charley has made its unexpected right-turn. So now instead of Tampa and its outskirts in hurricane-watch mode, the announcers on TV and radio tell everyone south of Tampa to prepare for the worst. Everyone's in complete panic! Charley could turn again, who knows? This was cosmic roulette with an insane killer-storm.

Even before midnight on the 12th, as Charley roared through Havana, no gas was available at filling stations within a fifty-mile radius of Tampa. Now, by 10 a.m. there won't be any fuel in any southern areas either, not in Sarasota, Venice or Fort Myers. By eleven there won't be any batteries or jugs of water left, just empty shelves in every neighborhood grocery store.

On the horizon, the sun was cracking on this unlucky Friday.

CHAPTER 4

she prayed me up

I'm awakened by the rustle of the massive, overhanging oak tree limbs that grow tall around our two-story house. They are shaking like demonic maracas in the pre-storm gusts now hurled at my inland hometown. Our teenage son and daughter sleep soundly through the warning gusts that have awakened only me. I guess I'm more sensitive to weather changes than most landlubbers, waking easily as blue-water sailors do whenever there's a wind or course shift.

In the pre-dawn darkness, I lie in bed alongside Will, my peacefully sleeping husband, listening, wondering, remembering.

I recall my first experiences with killer-storms. Many years before, I'd gone through two back-to-back hurricanes when I lived in Dominica, a tiny independent island country smack in the middle of the Caribbean chain. I recall how scary they were, two weeks apart, right on one another's heels, one eye directly hitting my tiny home island back in 1979. I'm lying in bed now, listening to the same screeches and howls foretelling what's soon to come. I remember Hurricane David, then Frederick, like a bad dream twice over. I'm resigned, waiting, knowing what comes next.

Yesterday, the day before the storm's direct strike was forecast for our area, the intermittent gusts were like trumpets blowing, whipping up the wind with sound and fury, creating high anxiety for the upcoming event. Adrenaline raced in everyone's veins who heard or felt the day-before gusts. The memory of what was coming hit me then, like a snowball in the face, when I went outside to do Reiki on my trees before driving to Bowling Green.

For all of Thursday, every other hour a *burp* would precede what Charley was readying to throw our way. I could smell trouble's stench in each consecutive gust. Out of nowhere, but always from the southeast, the previous day's gusts attacked from an innocent-looking blue sky. Because, still hundreds of miles away—Charley was a-brewin'. Huge gusts, from swirling invisible funnels, shot forward of the massive storm front, heralding the soon-to-arrive, hundred-mile-wide system. They blew hard onto the front of my car when I drove to and from teaching at the academy. More strong gusts intermittently tore at me that evening, when I walked outside every so often to check on the source-less howling. It was the wind moaning through every crack of our house. A reminder of David, Frederick, and the powerful thing coming next. I'd seen these preceding burps too many times to feel anything but out-of-my-skin expectant.

Miles away from where I was waking up on Friday, Ursula lay in her bed in St. Petersburg, some forty miles south of Tampa. A Florida girl since birth, Ursula too, has been through a few major hurricanes. Her house on the gulf coast is surrounded by the gentle fronds of tall but flexible palm trees, unlike the brittle hardwood trees of my inland home. Oaks are more easily toppled in high winds because they have no deep tap roots, and their woody limbs are inflexible. Ursula had been awakened by her infant's soft whimpers, in need of a feeding, not by a troubled mind haunted by near escapes of weather catastrophes as I'd experienced before.

After Ursula changes and feeds her baby Vrish, and he's been satisfied, she and her husband gather around the TV to hear the latest NHC (National Hurricane Center of NOAA, the National Oceanic and Atmospheric Administration) updates on Charley's expected arrival. She and Rafi her husband are shocked to learn Charley's radical path has changed during the night. On their TV screen they see the storm's drastically altered course since the time they went to bed. Now the massive system's eye is predicted to make landfall— not north of them as earlier predicted—but well south of their coastal town below Tampa Bay.

"We're in the middle of both predictions, last night's and today's," Ursula mumbles, dialing the academy. First she attended to her family, then she attends to her girls at ABG. She looks over at Rafi and both feel relieved by the news update. As Estelle's cell phone rings at the academy, Ursula, for the moment at least, thinks this storm's epicenter, the most dangerous part of every cyclone, just might miss St. Pete after all.

Rafi tucks their son back into his crib after his feeding and starts making breakfast as Ursula receives her first check-in from Estelle.

"Yes, the girls slept through the night just fine, don't you worry none, Miss Ursula," her trustworthy head guard tells her as she prepares for her usual day. Before she departs for ABG Ursula will once again feed Vrish, and pump a supply of her milk for when she's gone to Bowling Green, which she does even on the most miserable day. She drives the hours-long back-and-forth commute each workday. Since she stopped nursing her baby full time and started pumping, Rafi has taken over the baby's care during the day, per their agreement. They'd agreed that, for the first year of Vrish's life, one of his parents would always be present.

"I wonder if you should just stay home today, Urs," Rafi says from the next room as Ursula disconnects her call. "It's too risky to be making that long trip. And wouldn't it be ironic if—even though the eye might not hit us here—it hits Bowling Green? That would just be too awful. The girls are okay with Estelle on duty. She agreed to stay throughout the storm, didn't she?"

"Yes, she has no intention of leaving her girls. Not till the storm is well past them. And Mr. Eric too, he's volunteered to stay if we need him. But he'd prefer to be with his wife. They live nearby, so I told him not to worry, he can go home when he's secured the facility."

"There won't be any men at the academy?"

"Mr. Lawrence has agreed to stay."

"Well then, why don't you think about staying home, Urs. For me and Vrish? You know how hurricanes are. It could just as well be heading straight for Bowling Green as hit Tampa, or Naples."

"That's exactly what I was thinking, hon," Ursula says.

She picks up the cell and pushes the speed dial for Estelle.

Each workday Ursula is joined in her commute to Bowling Green and back, by three colleagues of the academy who live close to her. One is the other psychologist beside herself, an affable young man, Harry, who counsels the residents, as everyone calls the ABG girls. Her other two passengers are trained security guards, called *staff* at the academy. Ursula figures the word "guard" is too evocative of a prison setting, rather than suggesting the unique rehabilitative-home environment she's designed. So "staff," which Estelle heads, are not to be confused with other professionals like teachers, counselors, healthcare workers, or local caterers who deliver meals three times a day.

"Miss Ursula, I sure wish you'd come," Estelle exclaims the moment Ursula tells her she may not make the trip. "The girls are doing their best, but soon's they woke up and heard Charley's likely coming straight here, they're panicked. But my girls are more frettin' about their families than they are 'bout themselves, I give them that."

"I'll do my best to get there, Estelle," Ursula assures her. Ursula trusts Estelle like she would her own mother, especially when it comes to assessing the mood of the academy. "I'll check with Highway Patrol to see if the roads are clear enough to get to Bowling Green. Over here the winds are already pretty bad, the last report said they're up to twenty-five miles an hour. Every few minutes they seem to pick up."

"Well, let me know what you decides before we lose cell phone connection. You know how the power and land phones go first when storms are roarin' closeby. I gotta go, Miss Ursula. The girls are askin' questions."

As she replaces the flap of her phone Ursula sighs. She's torn, no doubt about it.

At thirty-five, no nonsense Ursula, blonde, athletic, well-traveled and highly educated, has already demonstrated she can tackle anything standing in her path. She met her Pakistani husband while they were students in London. Life in America, even in semi-enlightened coastal Florida, hasn't been as easy as it was in England for either Rafi or her. People of color and mixed race marriages face more stigma in the South than in more cosmopolitan parts of the U.S.

Ursula concentrated on Adlerian theory during her Master's studies in psychology. After her initial job as a "schlock shrink" in the school department, she designed the unique "prototype for rehabilitating" that she now oversees at ABG. Unafraid to tackle what others in the juvenile prison system (along with the Girl Scouts director, who referred to the "bad girls at ABG" as "incorrigibles") see as hopeless, this shrink—and new mother—balances her family's demands with being devoted to her teenage wards of the State.

As Ursula told me at our first meeting two years before, after she hugged me, "I prayed you up. That's right, I did. Juvenile offenders are the left-behinds of the prison system. I mean to change that. If we don't help these girls, and alter the way juvies are rehabilitated, at-risk kids, boys and girls alike, are going to spend the rest of their lives in and out of adult prison. The data has proven that. ABG is ground-breaking, and believe me, we need yoga and meditative mindfulness here just as much, maybe more, than mental health therapy."

I also quickly discovered at that first meeting Ursula was a practicing Buddhist. "In my own way, I meditate and align myself with the Divine," she'd said.

Ursula and Rafi's baby, even during her months of pregnancy, was an integral part of the four years of Ursula's direction at ABG. After the baby's first few months, on days when a hurricane wasn't threatening her angst-ridden residents, Ursula would often bring the good-humored baby with her to work. She allowed the girls to join her in feeding, changing and playing with Vrish, as if they were aunties and cousins, partners in the joys and hardships of mothering her newborn. Those who had babies of their own back home felt grateful, while those of the opposite variety kept their distance. Most of the girls at the academy loved Vrish, cooed and cuddled him, acting not the least bit like teenage criminals when Ursula's bundle of joy came for the day to ABG.

As director, Ursula created and secured funding for her unique program, an experiential approach to healing all psychic woes, not just in theory. At the beginning, the academy housed twenty-six addicted girls in one wing, but soon, twenty-six girls with mental-health issues joined them in a separate wing. Otherwise kept separate, once a day both groups were brought together in the common room for the daily House Meeting. Sponsored and partially funded by the State of Florida, the academy was Ursula's baby, long before she gave birth to Vrish.

For years Rafi had run his own construction business in coastal St. Pete, hours away. Yet he was willing to let his trusty workers carry on the actual building projects while he made the bigger decisions from his home office, making himself always available for his son's caretaking. He and Ursula had arrived at this arrangement when first planning their family. How many other sacrifices did Ursula make, I often wondered, to fulfill her dream of helping these former bad girls heal from their trauma?

Each of the twenty-six cramped but adequate bedrooms was shared by two girls. As the storm nears, every girl is lying sleepless in her individual bunk, listening to the howling wind outside her plastic safety window. I'll find out later it's only the yoga girls who are also listening to the sound of their own breath.

In this lockup facility, like all others nationwide, no inmate was ever allowed outside the tall chain-link fence without handcuffs and accompanied by a guard. No one ever escaped the surrounding fence, topped by lethal loops of razor wire. Even when the girls visited a dentist or doctor, handcuffs were mandatory. A country eatery-hangout in its last incarnation before Ursula found it abandoned, leased it, and thoroughly customized it as a juvie-detention, the cement-block fortress of a building, located in the tiny cattle-town hamlet that had one official street light at its lone intersection, was smack dab in the middle of nowhere. The nearly deserted ol' cracker town of Bowling Green, with no nearby major town or cultural center, not even a movie theater or Walmart, had nothing going for it, except ABG.

Ursula's crew converted the beat-up, rundown two-story, two-winged building into a secure lock-down facility to house the two different *types* of girls sentenced for repeated offenses. The most common of their transgressions was habitual use, possession, or selling of controlled substances. ABG's population was composed of habitual liars, car thieves, and drug dealers, plus a few who had committed more serious crimes, some for fabrication of crystal meth, known as *crank* in the South. One among the rowdy group had been charged with attempted murder (of her grandmother!) and others for assault with a deadly weapon.

The cement walls of the facility were twelve-inches thick. In the middle of the main building's two wings, which contained the sleeping quarters, was a spacious and carpeted, chair-lined large room where House Meetings were held, and also my two weekly classes. Adjacent to this common room, as it was called, for events that required the presence of all the girls, was the ballroom-sized, linoleum-floored cafeteria with its never-used full-size kitchen. Painted such cheery colors on the outside, with cottage-trim around the barred and thick plastic windows, the glass removed for security reasons, ABG had the appearance of a benign building in the one-light town. The user-friendly design was Ursula's anti-institutional choice. But she couldn't get the State to relax on the mandatory polyester uniforms the girls had to wear, with long tan slacks and short-sleeved navy blue stiff-collared shirts, ABG's logo emblazoned in lime-green over their hearts.

For the fifth time, Ursula hangs up from speaking with Estelle and looks out the window. Around her house the six tall palm trees, two 80-foot Washingtonians, two 50-foot Queens, and two Royals, are being tossed like salad greens, their limber trunks forced into bend-overs by the steadily increasing winds. Ursula can tell by the screeching outside, the wind has noticeably risen since she'd awoken an hour before.

Rafi calls Ursula into their living room. He points to the TV screen with the Weather Channel's radar beamed from a satellite. The images are changing as rapidly, as luridly as a flashing Vegas casino marquee.

Onscreen the newscaster tells of gusts coming off the system, climbing every hour.

"Erratic compass-jumping is happening, the latest from NOAA's Hurricane Center," the man announces in a Breaking-News serious tone. "We may have an official course change if the speed factor keeps pace with the system's forward thrust. Stay tuned, folks."

CHAPTER 5

the light within

Estelle wasn't kidding when she told Ursula, "I need help here, the girls are worried sick."

The girls are lucky to have her. They called the woman with skin the color of toasted coconut, *Miss* Estelle even though, at forty-nine, she's already twice a grandmother. During the previous two years I'd come up with my privately-dubbed monikers of "good and bad guards" for Estelle, obviously the better one, and Mr. Lawrence, the unfriendly guy with downturned mouth and lighter complexion. He's the one who stood out from everyone at ABG for his rotten attitude. He's the only one who never smiled, of the twenty-some trained guards on call to work, substitute, or be there whenever needed (every full moon, for instance). A minimum of four guards was needed when nothing special was happening, like at lights-out when the community of girls slept. Three staff were on call for extra security for every shift, meeting State and Federal requirements for the academy's population. Seven staff were required to oversee the entire community of fifty-two girls during a normal daytime shift. Five teachers for various classes, plus two mental-health counselors (Ursula being one), and an in-house nurse were all on site during an average school day.

Male and female guards underwent extensive training in dealing with unruly individuals who tended toward hysteria, practically the definition of a teenage girl. But they had additional skills, beyond that of supervising the girls. The guards—the staff of ABG—were also trained to do a *takedown* of a berserk, out-of-control inmate.

When I first witnessed this shocking event, I stood speechless watching what I thought was something I'd only seen in a hardcore-prison movie, never in my peaceful, yoga-centered real life. I was amazed it was only these seven staff that could manage this assortment of mentally challenged and gang-style druggy girls, every one of them pumped-up on adolescent hormones each day, every day. Sometimes when I visited, it just didn't seem there were enough guards for the raging going on.

From my home in Lackland, the academy seems even more understaffed on this Thursday, with Charley charging down on them. The girls of ABG must be—how could they not?—way more stressed than usual, because they are *always* stressed and full of all-consuming angst. I imagine the staff, headed by Miss Estelle and Mr. Lawrence during most day shifts, will be on their beepin'-buzzin' walkie-talkies now, even more than usual. They'll be placing nonstop phone calls to Ursula, I bet, and she'll probably call her supervisor to request staff reinforcements.

Everyone knows this isn't going to be any ordinary weird-to-start-with Friday the 13th. "Thank God it's the dark phase and not the full moon," Estelle tells Ursula over the phone. "I never seen my girls so riled up." She's grateful for this dark moon phase because she's well aware of the negative effect of the full moon. Something in the gravitational pull, she's heard, affects the seas as well as all animals on earth.

Even when they get over-the-top anxious, stressed and prickly as a bunch of cacti-people, Estelle calls them all *her girls*; both wings of inmates, equal in her eyes. Their rooms are never called cells or bedrooms. Of course, Ursula has to refer to the two groups of girls as separate in her official reports, but if Estelle must differentiate one from another on occasion, she calls them her "a-girls" for *addicts* and her "b-girls" for *behavior,* instead of m-h girls, for instance, for the category of *mental-health girls* Ursula had to use in her two separate reports. This is the only way Estelle ever acknowledges a separation between her two isolated sets of girls.

Every week girls sign up for my class, one held for each of the two groups. On paper my time with the yoga girls is officially referred to as a class for *Stress Reduction Techniques.* Ursula, who submits monthly reports for each segment of the program, shared with me that she once wrote that my teaching yoga and meditation there, "boosts not only the attending girls' self-esteem, lessening anxiety for each group of girls, but positively and noticeably influences the entire population, since the volunteer's very first class."

After a few months at the academy, Ursula cornered me as I was leaving, wanting to show me her monthly official report. She stood right beside me as I read, beaming at me.

"A new and unprecedented sense of peace has arrived at the facility since these classes have been offered. The individuals who are studying with Miss teZa are affecting the entire population. There are 50% less takedowns. Remarkably, a peacefulness is now discernible that previously never existed. This change in the overall attitude of the girls has been remarked upon by my entire staff since the yoga class started."

I was impressed. But when I read the next sentence, my big smile matched Ursula's.

"We are now offering a part-time position to hire this volunteer for her two weekly classes, as we feel her services warrant compensation."

Like every Thursday, I arrived at the tail end of the noonday House Meeting, always held in the common room, with our class immediately following. Every day at the same time, the combined population of both groups of girls convenes with their staff, to share about life, problems or achievements, or whatever else is on their minds.

In one of the corners of the large room—with its buttery-colored paint job, jammed wall-to-wall with comfortable sofas and upholstered chairs—is permanently displayed what Ursula calls "the girls' altar." On a low shelf so everyone can see the items, the girls are encouraged to place their own special found objects (really, the only tokens they can find in their barren environs, like pebbles, a candy wrapper, an occasional feather, a dropped hair elastic, a forgotten office paperclip). The girls cherish these offerings as well as their tightly folded notes garnished with hand-drawn flowers, stars, and smiley faces, also placed on the altar, requesting something, or expressing thanks. Miss Ursula taught them to use the altar for "speaking to your higher Self." Each day, stuck into a small blue bottle filled with water, set upon this easy-to-see shelf, would be a new dandelion, leaf or weed, bloom or seed pod found outside, blown over the screened fence, or fallen from a nearby tree. No matter what it was, each item was a *big deal* to whoever put it there on the altar. Each pebble could hold a dream; each weed, a locked-up teenager's reason for living.

The two groups of girls take their meals in two shifts in the cafeteria, at long Formica-surfaced tables with stackable metal chairs. Meals brought in from a local State-certified kitchen lessen the amount of people needed to cook, clean, and serve at the academy.

Several outlying trailers were squeezed onto the academy's limited fenced grounds the year before, after the number of inmates exceeded thirty. Before then, everything was contained in the main building. But Ursula's successful dual program expanded and room was needed for ten more teachers, counselors, and additional staff to oversee the girls' rehabilitative environment.

In Wauchula, ten miles distant, both Estelle's grandbabies, aged two-years and nine-months, are sleeping safely in their cribs this muggy Friday morning, as darkness is pierced by the light of a pewter dawn's soft glimmer. There's an opaque gray sky this morning because Charley is on its way. Safe in their own homes, Estelle's daughters' families are asleep. Many years divorced, Estelle lives alone in Zolfo Springs, near Bowling Green, but she spends more time at the academy than she does at home or with her daughters. After raising her son and two daughters by herself, all three now in their twenties, Estelle needs to be close to her *other* girls because, as she told Ursula, "My kids don't need me so much anymore."

Ursula doesn't have to ask Estelle to stay on past her usual hours. An extra shift for her seems like "the right thing," Estelle said, when Ursula noticed her helping out without being asked during this emergency. Estelle never considers going home after she and the other staff get the news that Charley has changed course—and its eye is officially heading their way.

If the massive system keeps its current position, Bowling Green is now directly in the *extreme danger zone*— the storm's very center, just a few miles wide—according to the latest report.

Estelle's not worried about her own children but focuses on her ABG charges. When they come out of their rooms after the 7 a.m. wakeup call she says, "Looks like we might be gettin' a little more than some wind and rain today, girls."

That Thursday, as I drove the long black ribbon of lonely highway to-and-from the academy, heading deep into the heart of central Florida's cattle country, I figured my two other Friday yoga classes, now also salaried—at Live Oak Academy, located in my hometown, another high-security State-run prison for youth offenders—would be canceled. But I never suspected that Charley's eye would actually head straight for Bowling Green. I'd been hired by the other facility after Ursula raved to her associates about the peaceful effects yoga had instantly brought to ABG's entire program.

Everyone at the academy was on edge, I noticed right away.

As I parked my car in the dusty lot and walked through the several sets of locked gates a guard had to unlock, I had no idea that tomorrow, Friday, would be the worst day of these young girls' lives. I'd already set the theme of this Thursday's class. So self-evident, I thought as I drove here, knowing that Charley was looming ever closer to us and ... that tomorrow would be the *big day* of its arrival in our area. I decided to use the threat of Charley's lurching toward us as the focus for that day's teaching.

"Fear of the unknown and what to do about it is our theme today," I announce as each class of yoga girls files into the common room, kept in order by Mr. Lawrence, his perpetually transmitting walkie-talkie and insouciant slouch as predictable as his scowl.

"Today we're going to practice how to stay in the calm center of our own Beingness, a place where nothing can harm us. Nothing can hurt us when we tap into our own power within. Remember?"

The girls respond with cheers and excitement, replacing the foggy, fearful looks on their faces moments before.

"Oh yes, Miss T! I remember you saying we can focus on something positive. Like the way my grandmamma loves me. And not let any bad thing at all get me down," Shay shouts. She's so enthusiastic that the others immediately switch gears as well—even if they hadn't remembered anything.

"That's right," I say. "So let's sit in our circle and start. We have a lot of calming down to do today. Tomorrow's going to be a very important day for all of us."

I look over at Mr. Lawrence who's made a sucking sound with his teeth. I realize he's not even aware of being as judgmental as he appears. "The poor unconscious fellow," I think to myself. Then quickly dismiss my unflattering assessment as just as bad as his negativity.

"Let's close our eyes as we start our yoga breathing, shall we? And slowly, with each breath in, let's remember how we can use the power of our inner strength to help us, especially tomorrow, to get through any of the scary things in life. We'll call this discovery of our own inner power, our inner 'I', as in *me, myself and I*. That's because within each of us, trust me, is the same power contained within the *eye* of this hurricane that's coming straight for us."

I pause a moment, then add, "Each eye of a hurricane contains the worst of the storm, yet at its very center—is absolute calm. Imagine that!"

I listen to the girls breathing in long and slowly, and breathing out the same way, always eager to follow my lead. Most have their eyes closed. We are instantly in a land of peace, having traveled together to this inner center so many times before. After a few silent breaths I quietly add, "They call it Charley, but don't for a minute underestimate this storm's extraordinary power because of its ordinary name.

"And just so you can remember to do this tomorrow, when Charley's here, today we're going to spend a little extra time in this quiet center within ourselves, our inner 'I'. That's why we're exploring it more than usual in our talking time today. You want to know ahead of time, so that, like, if the storm draws real near tomorrow, you can easily visit your own inner calm. Just as you can any time you want to. So let's watch our breath as we bring air in, that's right. And … watch the breath as we push it out. Slowly, each breath, the same in as out. You can count, if you wish. Breath in, two-three-four; breath out, two-three-four. Let's sit and watch the breath breathing us now, shall we?"

After a few minutes of complete silence and no movement, the girls start to stir. Each of the tan, brown or pink faces of now-seated, shifting girls—bound by the burden of their synthetically uncomfortable clothes as well as harsh court sentences—are transformed. They are now luminous with peace and calm. For the moment, each girl has completely let go of any fears, not just over Charley's imminent approach.

"You can slowly open your eyes, if you're ready," I say.

The girls turn to look at each other, realizing they're feeling the same weird calm they experience every week, breathing like this, sitting still like this. Everyone starts giggling. They know by now that this tall, lanky, henna-haired yoga teacher of theirs, old enough to be their grandmother but more agile than any girl there—probably has more tricks up her sleeve.

Again, I focus on the intention of the class.

"Girls, in the very center of each hurricane is an absolutely still center. It's called the eye. In the same way, within each person is a tranquil spiritual center. That place is our own inner *'I'*. To get to that secret *'I'* all we have to do is quiet our busy mind. How do we do that, girls? Any ideas?"

Kali has been coming to class the longest. "Concentrate on our breath," she says, and smiles knowingly. "Like we just did. Like we can do anytime we need to."

I sigh with joy. My two-year-long efforts have paid off, evidenced in this one comment of Kali's.

The girls go through the slowly executed sun salutes we always perform to warm up. I know it's Alex's next-to-last week. She's a white girl with dark hair, pulled back in a severe ponytail like every other long-haired inmate's. No one appears to be this girl's friend. With her struck-deer look, I never know if Alex/Durga will join us in the poses or if she'll sit in a corner by herself, always the loner. But right now, she's smiling, moving her trim and strong body in the series of twelve different asanas, our salutation to the sun. As I watch her well-practiced *surya namaskar,* I think of how often Alex has heard me reveal one snippet after another about myself. How I transformed from a confirmed bad girl to what I appear to be today, a happy-go-lucky yoga teacher.

"After beating myself up for all the bad choices I made when I was younger," I say, "I finally realized there was something more to life than feeling stuck."

The yoga girls are paying attention on this muggy afternoon, the temperature outside pushing the mercury up to 102 degrees. "Yeah, I've told you before, but for TraySea's sake, this being only her second class, I'll say it again: I was a teenage addict and hell-on-wheels, like all of you."

The regular yoga girls start laughing. I always say the same thing to every single new girl.

TraySea/Tara shakes her head in disbelief as smirks crack the faces of the regulars, looking at her classmates who nod and say, "She's right!," to confirm what I've just said—and our newest attendee's doubt instantly fades. There's no time for lying or mind-games in our limited time together.

I continue, "So you know what I mean when I say there's never enough booze, enough drugs, money, power—sex, acting badly, getting away with murder—'cause I tried it all and there's nothing but never enough. We end up in places like this; or institutions where we're sent if we lose our marbles. Or become homeless. Or forget the real adventure is on the inside, and never stop looking for it on the outside. We lose our joy, or meet our nemesis, a person who tries to ruin our life. Or we have an accident, an overdose, go too far. Then we either lose our life's purpose—or, even worse, our life, or someone else's."

The regular yoga girls keep nodding, knowing what I'm saying is all too true. They are proof, as I once was, of the dead-ends that bad choices always lead to. I drop hints here and there, just enough to keep them baited on my love-hook. How I've lived through all the whirling dark thoughts that crowd any human head, the demon winds that arise within each of us. Addictions to being negative, filled with judgment, intolerance, fear or anger over real or perceived personal injustices—even a nation's bad political pick—that, when not checked and altered, can lead to destructive thinking, self-sabotage, self-abuse, and limited relationships. For some, like these girls, their unhealthy addictions led them to crime. Negative, angry demons that are allowed to thrive in our consciousness unrestrained, will blow us away. Just like the hurricane will try to do that's right now roaring toward us.

"I'm just like you," I say, mainly for Tara's sake. "Only I didn't have the opportunity to change so early in life as you guys do."

I remind the girls I've been through *life-storms* as they have, calamitous whirlwinds of my own or another's making. They all nod their heads, knowing exactly what I mean—the bad choices and screw-ups, the depravity, the horrors.

"I didn't get caught and thrown in prison as young as you guys have," I repeat.

Anyone who didn't hear me mention this before looks at the others in disbelief. I've seen every girl react the same way when revealing my secret past. "It's like you can see inside our soul, Miss," I've been told many times in class.

I take a deep breath and return to the theme of class today.

"That's why it's important to make those demons behave, before they wreck our time here on earth. We do that by recognizing they're not real. They're just pretend, invisible, bad feelings left over from some other time, some other place.

"So today I want you to practice following your breath. We're going to journey together to our own powerful spiritual center within. Right inside us. Our Beingness. How? We watch the breath come in slowly, we watch it go out evenly. In the middle of our poses we watch it. Even in the middle of a conversation we can watch our breath. All day, every day we can do this. But we'll start with right now. One breath at a time.

"We'll focus on the steady, calming energy that our breath is, filling us with the life force, keeping us going, bringing us strength to persevere. Helping us to stay anchored in inner peace, no matter what happens on the outside. Tomorrow is a big day for all of us. You'll be much more comfortable if you remember to focus on your breath. Breath is the bridge to the Light within ourselves, our higher Self. Remember this and all will be well. Each and every moment, no matter what's happening on the outside. I promise."

the real adventure is on the inside

CHAPTER 6

what's in a name?

A major hurricane was due to strike sometime Friday. Everyone on the coast who was sane spent all day Thursday boarding up windows and securing everything loose outside.

The girls at ABG are understandably anxious, never having been in the direct path of a serious hurricane. But like anyone else who lives in Florida, they've skirted that possibility before now. These girls in lockup, however, have always been more concerned with either controlling others or getting away from others trying to control them. Learning how to be self-empowered is a new concept for all of them. They're eager to learn about this "power within" that we talk about in yoga class. They may not understand the impending disaster that's heading their way, but they like the idea of being in control of their own inner state.

They had no idea anyone could do that—control their inner state, their very Beingness—before coming to the academy. And now they'll experience, firsthand, how terribly awful controlling things can really get—and just from the weather!

☙❧

"How come you call her that?" TraySea demands when she hears me call Alex by her *yoga name*, Durga. Whether their given names are common or exotic—Lashonda, Vonquis, Tiffany, Christina,

Ashley or Katy—most girls ask for yoga names as soon as they "hit the mat" (yoga-speak for "doing yoga," but in this case, the only mat available at ABG is the motley indoor-outdoor carpeting of the common room, from which I protect the girls' faces by the clean washcloths I bring).

"It's something we do here in class," I explain. The girls liked it when I told them I made up my own spiritual name—on my papers, officially, it's L-teZa. So they all wanted to have a new spiritual name. "Miss Ursula says we can do that, but the name you choose is only for when we're here in yoga class."

I explain to TraySea how teZa came to be my spiritual name. "I use it to signify a starting-over time in my life. When I was ready to put down my bad habit of using mood-altering chemicals, decades ago, I changed it."

"And Kali's my yoga name," shouts the girl whose real name is Katy, even though she's often called *the absconder*.

"And I'm Matrika," shouts Tiffany.

"And I'm Maya," Sha'ria adds quietly.

We go around the circle. The girls share with our newest arrival the yoga names they'd chosen from the list I now offer TraySea. Each name had an English meaning printed next to it. Matrika is the *power of word;* Kali is the *destroyer of negatives;* Maya, *the illusion of reality.* Sometimes I'd forget a girl's yoga name, but they never did. It was a special treat to have a name they could choose themselves, something personally significant. Representing a quality about themselves they like.

From the time I first started teaching yoga here, almost every new girl who showed up in class wanted a new yoga name. It started with a girl named Linda after telling me she hated her name. She chose Dharma, which loosely means *the purpose of one's existence* when I offered her the choice of a couple Sanskrit names I knew off the top of my head. Then all the girls swore they hated their names, too. One by one each squealed delightedly when I suggested she take a new name for "this new approach to life we do in yoga and meditation," learning to *be empowered.* This Thursday Gail chose Shanti, meaning simply, *peace.* By the end of class TraySea announced she chose Tara, a Buddhist female-deity, meaning *inner strength.*

⚜

Along with name-changes came my first discovery about life here: there's a pecking order in lockup. Maybe more so than on the Outs. Ursula explained it to me this way, "This population of young girls demonstrates the persistent need people have, even teenage juvie girls, to control or be controlled. No matter how we try to discourage it, the population becomes divided into those who control—by either mental pressure or physical force—and those who try their best not to be controlled."

Everyone at this Thursday class has a yoga name. Katy chose Kali, *the fierce goddess who decimates evil,* because she often proudly boasts how she ran away while on a home visit on a coveted weekend pass she'd legitimately earned at the academy. She and her druggy boyfriend were on the lam for a week before she turned herself in. When she returned to lockup three months were added on to her sentence for punishment. But it took doing something so foolish for Kali to then throw herself into yoga, "So I can stay content," she'd tell anyone who listened. Tiffany, a.k.a. Matrika, the *sacred energy of words,* has two kids at home. Monica's yoga name is Uma, the *mother-aspect of the Feminine Divine*; she has one kid. Dark-eyed Kristina's name is Bhakti, meaning *devotion.*

Besides choosing special names we have other, regular yoga-related rituals. Any girl who attends class, either when she has her period or is in a shifty dark mood, is given permission to sit out class, one girl only. She sits in the area where Mr. Lawrence is sprawled out, at a student desk. Today there's no girl sitting out class, but on days when there is one she's encouraged to write out her feelings in our black-bound notebooks. Visibly changing from stormy-angry to smiling and Light-filled, a stricken girl sits and writes secret, deep thoughts to me, and later I respond, in our *Yoga Thoughts* book. At any time, not just when they're sitting out class, I encourage the girls to write questions, ponderings, poems, or simply whatever's on their minds.

Many of the girls who sign up for our yoga self-empowerment class experience real transformation, genuine and, to me, radical, for anyone in or out of lockup. The true test, certainly, will be when they're released, on the Outs. Can they maintain this connection to the inner power that they're learning about? The power within is mysterious; once ignited, it burns strongly.

Surely their young lives will be changed forever, having attended a class where they learn peace lies within all of us, no matter what's going on outside ourselves.

Later that Thursday night and on into the early morning hours of Friday, Charley rages on, exiting the north coast of Cuba around 2 a.m. Suddenly the phantasmagoric storm shifts, taking a sharp turn on the compass as hurricanes tend to do. Now—instead of Tampa, where everyone in Florida had been told to expect landfall, intensifying after its smooth spin over central Cuba—Charley abruptly changes course to a more easterly direction, just hours after leaving the island country.

Charley now is heading directly for Port Charlotte, one hundred miles south of Tampa.

The storm's official track is upgraded. TV and radio blast updates of the emergency announcement, the latest from the National Hurricane Center, the NHC out of Miami. News stories warn the population that the entire coastal area south of Tampa Bay, all of Charlotte County, and more precisely still, the area around Charlotte Harbor, is under a Hurricane Watch.

As soon as I awaken at home Friday morning, I know from watching the hurricane's updated, projected track that the worst, the most horrific brute force of Charley could now make a direct hit on the girls in Bowling Green in less than 24 hours.

In her restless sleeplessness, Estelle has gotten up from the cot she uses in her office when she's pulling an overnight at the academy. She drags her chair closer to look at the TV weather broadcast on the tiny portable set she keeps on her desk. She can clearly see, if Charley keeps churning toward land in the direction it now is going, the storm is making a direct beeline for her and her girls here in Bowling Green. She's glad they're all fast asleep in their skinny institutional beds.

It's 4 a.m. Four hours since Charley left Cuba. It's churning more easterly now. The winds have picked up as expected, over open ocean. "No longer is Charley the Category 3 it was as it ripped across Cuba," the Weather Channel says. "Now it's officially a Category 4 hurricane.

"We expect Charley to gather more tightly and increase in force before it makes landfall in Florida, somewhere between the Everglades and the Panhandle," the newswoman says as the screen shows a massive, out-of-control spinning top from a satellite's point of view.

Anything can happen. Just as hurricanes David and Frederick did years before, Charley could make a sudden right or left turn. Or do a complete about-face, like another innocuously named cyclone, Jeanne, who not once, but twice, slammed into the same area. Estelle looks at Charley's recent and sudden hop-jump on the radar screen, changing course by many degrees on the compass. A slowing down. A speeding up. The system noticeably gathering speed right before Estelle's wide, sleep-deprived eyes.

Estelle is appropriately scared. But she won't show it to anyone outside this sequestered room of hers. The NHC just announced Charley has been upgraded to a whopping Category 4, with 145 mph sustained winds.

"Jesus, Lord Almighty, this be serious," Estelle murmurs, shaking her head. "More wind than I ever been through, that for sure."

All of the Gulf of Mexico side of Florida wakes earlier than usual this Friday the 13th. Anything not done before, preparation-wise, in hopes the storm would head off somewhere else, now has to be done quickly. Roofs, boats, anything loose—must be battened down. Basic supplies like bread, milk, gas and bottled water are long gone. Soon nothing will be left on any shelf anywhere.

Home is where I am. Home is where Ursula still is deciding what to do. And her own home is where Estelle is not even giving thought to any more, not since the last NHC update. Her real home, for the time being at least, is with her girls at ABG. When we follow the projected track flashing before us on our respective TV screens, Ursula, Estelle and I can clearly see that the storm is heading straight for Bowling Green.

Floridians are now all awake. Everyone's heard. The storm is going to hit much more south than everyone thought when they'd gone to bed last night. All the official pre-storm arrangements had been put in place for Tampa Bay, several days earlier. Now Charley's aim is pointed way south, to Port Charlotte. Now people are panicking because the storm has done what they feared most—turned unexpectedly.

CHAPTER 7

open heart, open mind, easy spirit

E ven though Charley made an unexpected many-degrees turn around six that Friday morning, it wasn't until an hour later that TV and radio news announcers confirmed it. Only at 7 a.m. did preparations for Charley's much-more southerly landfall begin in earnest in places that the day before were believed safe.

The day before, Tampa Bay, St. Pete, and Clearwater were all prepared for the storm's lashing. Now, the people of the Port Charlotte area, a hundred miles south, are scrambling, evacuating, fleeing like surprised rats. Or staying and desperately shoring-up windows of homes and businesses, feeling hopelessly unprepared for the strike of Charley's last-minute-change landfall.

As soon as Ursula takes off for Bowling Green she wonders if she ought to turn back, stay in St. Pete, or at least bring her husband and baby with her. More than anyone she knows the facility is as strong as a bunker, with its thick cement walls and crash-proof plastic windows she'd had installed, required for all lockdown facilities. Plus, the building has a strong new roof, part of the academy's extensive renovations from, just a few years before, the dive called Elmer's Off the Beach, that run-down country hangout in gnat's-ass Bowling Green. She knows this because she, as the Mental Health director, has been involved with the birth of the academy since she first pitched its uniquely progressive idea of reform to the State's corrections department, an innovative, and in the long run, more cost-effective way of dealing with juvenile delinquents.

"Everyone wants to see success stories," Ursula had said, when presenting to the board her main premise. "Including a new approach to youth offenders' rehabilitation. Look at my studies," she explained, handing printouts to the committee she'd met with that day, five years earlier. "See the statistics on the notable success others have had with girls who are housed in dormitory-like living conditions, treated like the conflicted teenage students they are, rather than disrespected criminals. Now consider this data," she smiled, "and let me show you how to help these high-risk, low self-esteem teenage girls be saved from becoming lifelong antisocial repeat offenders."

Then Ursula handed out another sheet with this numbing statistic: *There are approximately 10 million Americans with mental illness and only 45,000 inpatient psychiatric beds. Jails and prisons are the nation's largest mental health care facilities.*

Ursula ended her presentation that day with these confident words: "When our youth get to know themselves better, we'll have fewer criminals to reform."

Soon afterward, she received final approval from the State of Florida for her funding, and ABG was born, from little more than a dream Ursula held strongly in her heart.

Ursula was the one who'd found the abandoned building in Bowling Green. Its previous occupant had been announced on billboards in the pastoral countryside, and over its entrance still hung the faded sign featuring a scantily clad bikini-babe waving at passersby, pointing the way to Elmer's Off the Beach—where no beach was to be found for seventy miles.

Ursula knew exactly how strong the building's thick cement walls were, how shatterproof each of its new windows, with bulletproof plastic preventing escapes or break-ins. And now, she hoped it would withstand a hurricane's brutal force. Ursula knew no other structure, besides an in-ground bunker, dug in a backyard, could provide the same protection as ABG's solidly built, high wind roof-ties and extra-strong construction bolts, offering maximum protection from gales and loose-flying objects.

She wondered how her charges were taking the news. How noisy the breakfast room was, with the two shifts of girls eating right about now.

Ursula was conflicted yet she continued driving under a thick overcast sky, over the Sunshine Skyway, south to Brandon where she caught Route 62 going east toward Bowling Green. In the passenger seat and in the back seat were Ursula's co-workers she took each workday to the academy.

The ride is tense. Everyone's conflicted: What's the right thing to do? Everything is so unpredictable. Nobody knows for sure what the storm is going to do. The nearly two-hour trip from her home in St. Petersburg to Bowling Green is usually more cheerful. Ursula looks in the rear-view mirror and catches the eye of Harry, her assistant shrink. In that instant, both of them wonder what the other is thinking. Ursula keeps her gaze on the slick, rainy road. Visibility is poor, with the next cloudburst that's just dumped on them. The wipers are going full blast, but the windshield is foggy, making the road hard to see. They are only thirty miles out of St. Pete, where all four passengers reside when they're not at their eight-hour shifts for the academy.

The car radio interrupts with a bulletin. The calm voice of the announcer says, "The Hurricane Center in Miami has just upgraded Charley's predicted path to right up the Peace River from Port Charlotte Bay, folks. After landfall, hurricanes often follow natural land indentations such as riverbeds."

Ursula knows what this means. Instead of feeling safer going to the academy, she's suddenly overcome with worry about her and

Rafi's little family, plus her own safety, because she's heading straight for the most dangerous part of the state.

Ursula has to say it. She starts to slow the car as she speaks to her car mates.

"You know guys, I'm sorry, but I don't think this is the right thing to do, heading for where the storm's heading. Leaving our own families right now. This report confirms our earlier suspicions, that Charley's now going straight toward the academy. I know the girls really need us. Maybe you all feel the same, but I'm inclined to turn around right now. The road's already flooded, and there's bound to be trees down soon. What do you think?"

The other three in the car voice their relieved agreement with Ursula; she spoke aloud what had been playing ping-pong in their minds.

"Estelle can hold down the fort," Ursula tells them as she pulls over on the empty highway. No other soul is traveling inland today. Everyone is home, burrowing in like people are supposed to do, like all animals do, seeking shelter before a big storm hits.

In the quiet as Ursula turns the car around they listen to the announcer adding what everyone fears: "The storm's path can shift position at any time."

Betty, an administrator who sits on Ursula's side, speaks up. "Let's call Estelle so she'll explain to everyone why we can't be there."

Ursula heads her blue Honda back toward St. Pete and hands her cell to Betty, who punches the speed dial. Focusing on the difficult driving conditions Ursula says, "If this storm keeps going on its present course, we'd be headed right for where *it's going*. That last NHC update did it for me." She looks at Harry in the mirror as Betty waits for Estelle to pick up. "Right for Bowling Green," Harry concurs.

In an hour, after dropping her co-workers at their homes, Ursula pulls back into her home's vegetation-covered driveway. Everything is littered with debris from the distressingly wild wind. Loose palm fronds have been yanked from their trunks by gusts of nearly fifty mph winds, now coming in steadier intervals. Before she shuts off the car the radio announcer assures his listeners that, if Charley keeps to its present course, the Tampa Bay-St. Pete area will only get the mild side of things.

Ursula can't help but sigh in relief. At least for now, her family won't face the worst conditions the storm will be dishing out. The not-knowing, the waiting, all the not-in-control anxiety of living through a massive, deadly storm, is starting to wear on Ursula's nerves. She holds her big day-bag tightly to her chest and rushes into the house, and without a word, right into her husband's study to check on their sleeping infant in his crib alongside Rafi's desk. Ursula then bends over her not-surprised husband to give him a long, tight hug as he sits at the computer's glowing screen.

They hold each other for some time, in the terror of Nature's wrath soon to alight. Fear grips all human hearts in Florida this Friday.

For the previous forty-eight hours it was Tampa residents, not Port Charlotte's, that had made extensive preparations. The storm has done its double-whammy on its unsuspecting victims, again! Mocking what authorities had predicted for its eye's landfall, the deadly epicenter of every hurricane, Charley's sardonic laughter could be heard high above the screeching, deafening witch-wind now accompanying the intermittent, no-standing-upright force. Charley is soon to arrive. Expectation sits like gelled glue in everyone's guts.

Ursula makes another call to the academy.

"Miss Ursula," Estelle's slow drawl comes crackling over the landline. "The girls sure sorry to hear you not coming, but we get by; don't you worry none. You just stay with that baby of yours and we be good. The girls and me, and all the staff here, we got what it takes to get through this nasty mess."

Ursula gets off the phone and mumbles a few words to herself, distracted. She's concerned about the safety of her girls, but she's also worried about her own family. She utters a few prayers for protection, and trusts that'll help. "A few words of gratitude will be forthcoming," she promises to no one, "soon as this is over." She's glad for Estelle's willingness, her eagerness, her efficiency and her bravery, and most of all, her commitment. Ursula silently asks the Powers That Be for protection, but also for the girls not to freak out too badly.

She knows this will be the greatest test of their lives. The eye of Charley—aimed right at them. Not some jealousy-born drama, a life-storm, or nasty repercussions from society for the girls' own wayward actions, or their parents' lack of care, or others not stepping in. Because now it's looking like, strongest building in the world or not—the academy is going to be getting one hell of a beating before this day is over.

With fury in its heart, ol' Charley's eye is headed straight for the girls in tiny Bowling Green.

Soon, at quarter to four in the afternoon, Charley starts pummeling Sanibel and Captiva, the outermost barrier islands just off Port Charlotte Harbor. Evacuations have been hurriedly enforced. Everyone who wanted to leave had to abandon their homes and businesses by noon. The storm surge, the NHC says, is expected to not be as bad as it could, because of favorable tide, wind and moon conditions that are making Charley's crash landing less damaging than predicted.

As Charley strikes the barrier islands, this event sets a macabre record. Just twenty-two hours earlier, Tropical Storm Bonnie had pummeled Florida's northwestern coast. Freakily, two massive systems colliding with the peninsular landmass of Florida within less than 24-hours sets a meteorological hallmark, one that most people throughout Florida will be happy to never know.

At the academy, the girls have just been told by Miss Estelle that Miss Ursula has decided, "after a lot of thought, to stay home today, with her baby boy and husband.

"Now girls," Estelle tells them at the general meeting she's called in the common room, "there nothing to fear. We be fine any old way it goes. Miss Ursula done tried, but the roads are bad and gonna get worse." Every girl regards Miss Estelle as the "mother of the academy," while they call Miss Ursula "the boss lady," mostly because they spend substantially more time with the older woman.

Estelle continues addressing the population. It's just before lunchtime.

"We have everything we need, right here," she points to her own heart. "We have our own love, and God love, too, protecting us. And these strong walls." The girls giggle, they are nervous. Titters and constant shuffling indicate that they are more restless than assured. Like the weather outside. "You got any questions, girls?" Estelle asks.

"Yeah," one girl speaks for everyone, "where we going to be, I mean, which room, through this damn Charley?"

"We gather here again, in the common room, when and if Charley gets closer. We safe here. We move further inside, to the cafeteria, if things get really bad. We surrounded by four solid walls there, not an outside wall of windows like here's in the common room. This older part of the building got thicker walls. And we have the second floor above us. Just in case."

"Just in case of what?" another asks.

"Don't you worry none. We have everything took care of, that be all you girls need to know. Anything else?"

"Can I call home to see how my mama and my baby are doing?"

"I sorry, girls, we gots to keep the lines open. Besides there no need for out-calls, you not hurt or sick. Unless someone from your family calls the office, this be an ordinary day with just a big storm coming. You know the rules. Tomorrow you have plenty of time for callin', after the weather clears up. Any other questions?"

No one raises their hand. The girls are dismissed, more sullen than usual, more anxious than their regular off-the-charts levels of stress. The storm has already created a thick fog of fear over the facility, though Estelle tried her best to dispel it.

Per Ursula's instructions the schedule will continue as usual, until it can't. Everyone on staff will attempt to keep the girls' routine as close to normal as possible. Until—and if—the eye bears down. Then the plan Ursula and Estelle worked out will be enforced. Meanwhile, Mr. Eric, the ever-smiling handyman at the academy, keeps busy as the girls cycle through their regular activities. They hear him on the outside as he screws sheets of plywood over any vulnerable spots, a weakened door here, a loose shutter there.

At home, I'm wondering how my students are faring on this momentous day. I'm confident I've given them enough mental and spiritual ammunition to get through anything. With all the inner work we did yesterday, TraySea/Tara and other girls who've been coming for weeks and some—like Kali and Durga, Shay and Maya—for months, will have all they need to remain calm, and perhaps even watch in awe the tremendous force of Nature they are about to experience. About half of the girls in attendance yesterday I consider seasoned yoginis—for being incarcerated teens, that is.

I've just come in from outside where I've been extending my hands, focusing my intention—sending my spiritual energies of protection—on the tall oak trees that surround our family's split-level. My spirit is clear, ready for yet another storm. Yesterday was a snoozer; I even traveled the gusty road to Bowling Green to teach. Yesterday the tail end of Bonnie, a much smaller system than Charley, never went beyond the tropical storm category for more than a few hours, little more than the garden-variety, usual fierce thunderstorms common in our area. Early at dawn yesterday Bonnie hit Lackland, and hissed like a scared cat through the rest of the middle of the state. All our storm supplies and hurricane supplies are still in place. The plywood's still up on our big windows, a precaution we take for any storm over seventy mph. Will and I and our two kids have been through this drill countless times before, and I've been through it even more times back in the West Indies, when I was always getting smacked around by stormy wind and water, and a few political catastrophes, too.

On Thursday, a few of our neighbors' old and weak trees were felled in the wind, but they needed pruning anyway. Our house stood strong, unscathed but for the messy branches, twigs and leaves that go everywhere in storms.

So again on Friday I'm doing my thing outside. "This Reiki works," I speak aloud as I extend my palms, shooting protective energy out to the tall and majestic trees that stand sentry around our vulnerable house. I transfer my feeling of strength to our woody guardians in Charley's quickly approaching wrath.

At that moment, 4:30 p.m., Charley is slamming full force into Port Charlotte, a town warned too late, a huddle of humans totally unprepared for such a fierce onslaught.

to feel connected ... go within

CHAPTER 8

the altar of assistance

Three extra staff have been called to help the seven regular guards keep order at the academy. Ursula made the necessary phone calls from her home, but she was confident that if her phone system failed, Estelle would have called out for extra help, as the two women already discussed this contingency—just in case—during one of their phone calls. When any day is filled with more tension and unpredictability than normal, Ursula requests three extra staff. The same procedure is followed for every full moon night when, predictably, the girls always act out. Usually, as a group, even on a "good day" the girls are restless. But when stress levels rise higher, from either full moons or another disturbance, there's always more than the usual number of takedowns.

Since they woke to the news that a tempest was headed their way, the majority of girls have been like walking zombies, in shock at hearing a major Force, something completely unprecedented, is on its way. They've had many tense times before, a riot even, when the entire community went on a rampage. Or an individual has freaked out over an in-prison romance, or a family event on the Outs she can't control. The full moon can make everyone go berserk. But with Charley's eye now on them, it's a different matter, it seems to Estelle. To her, it's the worst possible scenario imaginable, worse than all other bad times combined.

"I'm telling you, Miss Ursula," Estelle says in the next of the calls they've steadily made since morning. "I be impressed with our young things. I would never thought it, but these girls not misbehaving at all. They be so quiet I'm wondering if they in shock, being extra-special nice and sweet to each other. Like they know they make things worse by acting out. We got enough on our hands with gettin' ready for this storm fixin' to charge us, to do takedowns if we had'a, uh huh. But judging the girls' behaving so good, you wouldn't know an emergency situation is about ready to happen."

"I'm relieved to hear that," Ursula says.

"And you know it be funny, 'cause it seems them yoga girls bein' the calmest of the bunch. Like they have a ring of peace all 'round them and it be spreading to the others. I see how they helping calm down upset girls. But no one be misbehaving, not at all."

Ursula said, "It sounds just like the time we had the riot and the yoga girls were the only ones who didn't participate."

"Yes'm. Sure seems so. It be awful nice to see, all that peaceful work they do, paying off."

"Yes, it is," Ursula laughs. "Plus, it's been proven that crises make us humans more human." Ursula is greatly relieved to say what she's been feeling, especially after hearing Estelle's latest report of the girls good behavior, now of all times. "Shame we need a catastrophe for people to realize how nice we can be to one another, isn't it, Estelle?"

"Well, seems so," Estelle replies, "'cause these girls be helping each other today when usually they do nothing, and I mean, nothing. Maybe today they worried about their families and friends on the Outs in harm's way more than they concerned 'bout them own selves. It be a first, my seein' them like this."

Nobody knows, ever, what a storm is going to do. A storm could be a metaphor for life in general. Usually Ursula drives through any bad weather, thunderstorms, hail as big as golf balls, torrential rain that's common to the Florida's weather patterns. But today—after hearing the latest news flash, that the land-bouncing storm's path is on a course straight for her girls at the Academy of Bowling Green, right up the Peace River corridor—Ursula is glad she turned back and decided to stay home with her family. She knows the girls would like her there at the academy, if she could speak with them, but she's totally comfortable with Estelle's handling it all on her own.

Sheets of rain, relentless wind, swirling vegetative and human detritus, and wrenched-off roofing materials whoosh outside their un-boarded front window. The storm's eye, the TV news announcer says in their St. Pete living room, has left the metropolitan area of Port Charlotte in tatters. Boats, lifted up onto faraway streets; office windows, broken and papers blown away, sucked out of files and drawers. What few people were left in town are just glad to be alive.

Charley is now halfway to the small town of Fort Ogden, 13 miles inland from the devastated Charlotte Harbor with its many barrier islands, and the adjacent city of Punta Gorda. It's 5 p.m. Charley's slow but steady march across the mainland of Florida has begun.

At home, located well off the eye's predicted path, I sigh my relief after hearing the NHC's latest update. Our household is prepared. We have our Scrabble board out, and camping lanterns are by our sides if the power goes out. Yesterday, Bonnie's eye went way north of us, creating only mild rustles in our big oaks' limbs. Still, our family spent a couple hours yesterday, during the worst of that milder storm's battle with land elements, sheltered in our safe living room. The big sliding glass doors were darkened with plywood shields, and the rest of the windows had all been taped with giant Xs. The bathtub was filled with water, just in case; flashlights and candles were on hand, our two cars' tanks had been filled before every gas station within a fifty-mile radius ran out, well before Charley's actual course was clear. Ours, like all Florida families, knows how the hurricane drill goes.

Our home and family are ready for today's storm, a more dangerous situation. Once again I am standing outside, sending a shield of energy to the oaks. I'm thinking of Ursula, a cherished friend now, not just the director of the academy. In this quiet space before all hell breaks loose, I reflect on how she, with her expanded vision and open heart, single-handedly created the academy. I think of the girls in lockup, especially my yoga girls, who hungrily, eagerly lap up all I share with them about the miracle I feel life is with a meditative yoga practice at its core. I think about the non-yoga girls at the academy, too, and wish I could dive into their hearts and give them the gift of inner peace, teaching them, like the girls who come to class, how to love this sacred space as much as I do. Because the biggest reward of all in having a regular practice, along with the strong and limber body I now have, even in my mid-fifties, is the center of calm—even in the face of life's worst events. Developing a yoga and meditation practice has bestowed Self-love and a love of life upon my previously whacked-out, imbalanced life.

I know over at the academy they're preparing for potential disaster. Standing between the two tall oaks, I close my eyes.

I send my energy, what some call Reiki, to all the girls at the academy. This energy is to help them be strong, not afraid, and to know that they are safe. Even though now a real monster, the killer-hurricane named Charley, is heading right for them.

I visualize the community altar in the academy's common room then, where I hold our two classes each week. I smile, thinking of Ursula's encouraging each girl to place something special there to signify whatever they wish. A rock, a hair elastic, a leaf, some lint, a bit of paper, something, anything they want to offer as a token of giving and receiving power. From the invisible source. To help ease their suffering. An altar of Assistance.

The altar symbolizes what the academy itself attempts to do in each of these girls' lives, to empower them. To help them focus on good new habits and let go of the old bad ones that got them in trouble. To make better choices.

I stand for a while in silence, visualizing my energy surrounding the academy, helping whoever is there, Estelle and Mr. Lawrence and the other staff, all the girls, Mr. Eric, maybe. My energy is buzzing as I feel it strengthening the girls right now. My own family is well protected. We have plenty of support and assets, even though we face the normal challenges all families do. But for the residents of ABG, yoga- and non-yoga girls, druggie and mental health inmates alike, all of them desperately lonely or lost, feeling bereft of love and hope, many of their families locked in the destructive cycle of fear and addiction—they need all the help they can get.

Listening to the wind I remember how I was inspired to reach out to teach needy girls because my own stepdaughter, for whom I'd been the only female nurturer since she was seven, turned against me. When Kara reached puberty she started to hate my guts, buying into the shameful falsehoods her bio-mom had been feeding her since I'd first showed up in her kids' lives.

For some reason Kara's brother Jonny never fell under the spell of suspicion that his dear mama successfully used to draw Kara to the dark side. From the moment I became their *Angel Mom,* Jonny and Kara had trusted I was a good person. We never experienced any conflict—until the moment Kara set her teenage heart against me. Since then, nothing I could do or say could bring back the love she'd so joyously, so spontaneously expressed for me during our first seven years together after marrying her dad.

So now the yoga girls at ABG are the recipients of all I'd been so dearly wanting to share with my own *Angel Daughter*, who wanted nothing to do with me. And wouldn't until more than a decade later, after her own divorce, when she found herself hoping a good stepfather for her own child might appear one day. Funny how life goes in circles, isn't it?

I laugh when recalling how my athletic mother came to visit me once, and accompanied me to Bowling Green to observe her youngest daughter, an instructor to the residents of this high-security lockup. As we left the facility to return home that day, many months before Charley, my mom said, "Why teach them yoga? Why not calisthenics?"

Now, you'd think someone whose daughter has been doing yoga since her teens, just a little older than Kara, would understand, wouldn't you? But my mom knew nothing about yoga, or meditation, nor did she care to. "Bunch of hocus-pocus," she'd say if others brought it up, remarking how I stood on my head endlessly, in silence, whether in the backyard of my folks' home, or poolside when we'd visit friends. I'd done yoga wherever, whenever, since forever. But my mom had no concept of what I did other than that I didn't turn out the way she'd wanted.

She, on the other hand, was a golfer, a swimmer, and didn't see the need for "that weird stuff." This visit of hers to ABG, in fact, was the first time my mom had ever witnessed a yoga class. As she and I left the facility to return to Lackland, my mother questioned:

"Why yoga? Seems to me they need jumping jacks and push-ups more than this Eastern mumbo-jumbo," she curtly announced. I sighed, thinking how much more the girls got out of my offering yoga than they would—yes, I know this is true—art classes, another of the great loves of my life.

It was hard for mom having an always-different daughter who'd started doing yoga when she went to college in Boston. On the way out to our car, Mom stopped to offer another of her *comments*, which to me always felt more like *criticisms*. After a lifetime of feeling put down by these harsh observations, the self-awareness of a yogic approach had helped me to detach from my mom's rejection of who I was.

Mom came to a dead stop, planting her shoes firmly on the ground, and asked again, in a sharper tone, "Why not jumping jacks, honey?"

Right then, I noticed her open-toed shoe was pointing directly at a heart-shaped piece of gravel. It popped out at me like a limestone billboard. I stooped and picked up the stone, without answering mom's question. I knew better than to get into it with my mother, whose opinion had no room for anyone else's. Instead, I brought that special rock back to my own home altar, where I keep many of the heart-shaped rocks I've gathered over the years. On my altar, a shelf in Will's and my bedroom, I placed that large gravel heart-rock that mom's toe had pointed to, in recognition that no one's criticism, not even my own mother's, can hurt me anymore.

Just as Ursula urged all her girls at the academy to use symbols on their group altar, I too, as many students of consciousness do, use rituals such as altars, Reiki, and visualization, to combat my own inner demons. This heart-shaped rock lying beside Mom's shoe, would now hold a special place on my private altar—signifying another step toward freedom from others trying to steal my inner peace.

No one, not my mother nor my daughter, not any stranger, politician or bad-news event, has the right to control the inner peace I've worked so hard to find and keep alive in my heart.

CHAPTER 9

control vs. letting go

To my mother, I said, more to myself than to my chronic criticizer: "We all need to remember to reach for our highest self. Yoga is the best way I've found to do this. The poses teach me to balance and heal, by acquiring strength, patience, determination, flexibility. Learning to trust our body as the teacher it is—by listening to the inner wisdom all of us have within—leads to surrender."

My mom interrupted, "Surrender? What are you talking about? I'm asking you about helping these poor misguided girls!"

"I know, Mom. And I'm explaining why yoga works better than anything I've ever tried to feel good about myself. When we trust our bodies' ability to become as powerful as the practice of yoga makes it—we are surrendering to our own inner power."

Mom didn't like where this conversation was going. So she waved her open hand at me—as if she were swatting a fly midair, batting away this buzzing annoying thought—and got into my car, remaining sullen and withdrawn all the way back to Lackland.

As we drove I tried unsuccessfully to break the funk my somber mother was in. I gave her space and let my thoughts drift. I remembered the short demonstration class I'd given at ABG, attended by every single girl who crowded into the common room, standing less than arm's length apart. Some were interested in *weird yoga*, as they called it; many weren't interested in the slightest. With Ursula grinning like a loony lady, standing tall amidst her charges, taking the sample fifteen-minute class along with everyone else, I recall telling them that day:

"In yoga, we become victorious when we surrender to our own bodies' abilities. That's why we do breath-work and the poses. We don't fight our bodies, or try to control them. We surrender to the Power within, through the discipline of yoga. We make an effort, and we're at ease. Both of these happen at once in yoga. That's what the word yoga means: to unite. Effort and ease; body, mind, and spirit. When we engage in this discipline, we receive tremendous benefits. Our body becomes a well-maintained, so-called *holy temple*. Yoga is a Sanskrit word and means yoked, as in joined-to, the way an ox is yoked to an old-fashioned plow. When yoga is done correctly, we become better people. That's what this physical-mental-spiritual discipline will do for you."

From among her charges, Ursula loudly added her agreement after I ended the short session with a quiet time. We were all sprawled out on the floor. Somehow, all of us fit, head to foot, in that space. I encouraged each girl to listen to her own breathing. "This," I explained to them, "is meditation. A stilling of the busy mind. Watch your breath, just for a few rounds."

As the girls awoke from their minutes-long near-slumber, Ursula ended the demonstration by saying, "Girls, this is what I've been telling you about! How to get hooked on a healthy addiction. Yoga is definitely one of the good addictions, like respect and kindness, things that are going to make your life happier."

The girls lined up to return to their schedule after the short demonstration. Ursula continued speaking in a loud voice.

"Yoga has a side benefit. It releases endorphins like crazy, like running does. You've heard of *runners' high*? Endorphins are the brain's own natural, get-high hormone."

Astonished, the girls chuckled. Ursula raised her voice above the noisy din. "Instead of struggling with your bad addictions, try yoga, it's a good addiction. Right, Miss teZa?"

During classes I offered hints of what awaits those who continued to sign up. "The poses help us make better choices because they demonstrate our ability to achieve something—like a challenging balancing pose—all by ourselves. We don't need anyone else to do a tree, an eagle or a warrior pose. We learn how to position the limbs of our body. Sometimes I ask myself what pose I need to do in the moment, for a particular situation or emotion, and in that intuitive process alone, I become more focused. Just asking ourselves these questions we become more aware. We develop a sense of *being in tune*.

"Yoga is a way for our bodies to become our own teachers. We learn how to pray with our bodies, by linking our intention with our breath. The poses teach us to be powerful, not powerless. For all of us, in our unique relationship with life, we are happier when we feel more powerful about ourselves. In yoga, we learn the enormous power we can have over our own selves. You know how uncomfortable it is when we don't feel true to our self. That's because we lose our natural balance, our personal power, when we give away too much. We become weak when we don't protect and nurture that God-given birthright of our inner power. Our Beingness. The inner *'I'*.

"With yoga, we become powerful by learning not to let others control us. We alone control our own thoughts and our bodies. So we learn to control our own bodies even better, awesomely so, by doing these poses. By not letting outside situations steal our happiness, we stay in possession of our own power. Focusing on the strength we all have within—especially when our bodies are in a pose—we become much more than what we were without the body-mind awareness that yoga cultivates.

"Breath and balance, mind and body," I say at every class, "this is the essence of yoga."

I looked over at my mom who was feigning interest in the passing landscape as we sped toward Lackland. I knew from experience she'd scoff if I spoke about these aspects of yoga, so I kept quiet and recalled happier times in practice sessions with the girls.

"Making wise choices is the road to happiness," I'd say as the girls looked at each other, highly suspicious that I was nutso. No matter, I was used to people thinking me an oddball because I'd been doing yoga since my own teens. Back in the late sixties hardly anyone did yoga. Wherever I went, I'd draw a crowd of gawkers when I practiced in parks, beaches, rest stops or boat docks wherever I traveled.

As mom and I drove home that long-ago day I smiled, thinking of how Ursula always encouraged her girls, saying, "Doing time doing yoga will make your stay at ABG a pleasure instead of a pain!" Her head would bob up and down as she enthusiastically cheered the girls on, her grin as big as a cosmic clown's.

Back to the present on this Friday in August. Charley's eye is demolishing every tiny hamlet in its wake as it slowly crawls up Route 17, following the Peace River. All the house roofs in the eye's way tremble and some peel right off. A well-built factory outside Arcadia is flattened, its steel I-beams twisted like ribbons on a boxed present, flung far from where they kept the structure in place. Every deciduous tree within twenty miles of Charley's blender-radius eye is knocked over. People who chose not to evacuate are terrified, fearing for their lives, hunkered down in safe rooms, closets, bathrooms, praying to not be killed by this angry sky-creature shrieking around them, blowing away their lives, their homes, their minds.

As I busy myself with chores, waiting for the storm to dump its demon winds on us, the rest of my family are elsewhere in the house. I'm standing in front of my altar staring at the heart-shaped piece of gravel my mother's foot had once pointed to. My mind is suddenly flooded with other memories of the academy.

How I felt my heart race when I returned to my car in the lockup's shaded, gravel parking lot after the first demonstration I gave. It was obvious how badly the girls needed to become familiar with the power within. The same power lies within every living thing, as my teacher taught me so many years before, when I was first discovering it for myself.

It was only after I'd crashed and burned, like these at-risk girls have, that I finally learned about *The Choice*. Either live the half-life of a victim, or find out how to tap into one's inner power. Fortunately for me, when I was ready—the teacher appeared. Even though I'd been doing hatha yoga for my bad back since my teens, it was only after having come too close to death in my middle thirties that I chose to know my inner Self, the deep '*I*' within.

With that initial demonstration class, two years before Charley's rampage, I was introduced to a typical day in the academy.

Seven staff of both men and women kept order for the girls, the hardest challenge of every prison environment. Usually this meant that everyday there were one or two incidents necessitating a procedure of an extremely disturbing nature, to stop an individual from acting out.

It's unsettling for an outsider to witness a takedown. Freaked me right out when I first saw this radical maneuver. I didn't have a clue what was happening; I hadn't been forewarned. All I saw were the soles of a girl's shoes sticking out from a pile of three or four adult staff, who gently leaned sideways on her in a collective, calming influence, each one's weight firmly planted on the floor.

Naively, I asked "Can I help?"

The staff in the takedown shooed me away. I quietly asked another nearby staff what was going on and discovered *this* was "a PAR" (Protective Action Response) takedown.

I was told that when a girl didn't gain control of herself after being given a warning, if she continued to act out, she was deemed a threat to herself or others. At this point she'd be encircled by those trained in this maneuver. If the girl still didn't respond to requests to stop misbehaving, three or four staff would take her to the floor by a swift hand-to-shoulder, hand-to-hand pull-down, looking more like a group dance than a restraining technique used in prisons throughout the nation.

The staff members then lean their combined body weight against the hysterical girl who is now face-down on the floor. The staff stay in this position, talking to her, trying to soothe her, until the girl has settled. Sometimes it takes only minutes, sometimes much longer. The takedown is highly effective in maintaining order in a potentially volatile atmosphere, Ursula later told me. "Here, at any given time, any of the girls can lose control, start screaming, and hurt herself or others in a multitude of ways. We use the takedown to keep the peace. It's just part of life at the academy."

What can set off a person in detention? Sometimes it's as simple as a phone call from home. Or no call when one's expected. Other times it's the fear of going home soon—being on the Outs—or getting time added to their sentence, after having amassed a certain number of *criticals* for doing something stupid in lockup. A *critical* is an official offense, kept on record. Sometimes a girl goes bonkers, provoked by an in-jail jealousy, a discovered infidelity on the Outs, a word, or even a look from someone misconstrued as a putdown. Girls go wild over love gone bad or unrequited, or any other emotional upheaval.

Ursula blames most of ABG's takedowns on "raging teenage hormones."

A takedown isolates potential or actual trouble. When it's enacted (to stop combustible situations from escalating) everyone not involved—inmates and staff—are removed from the area. Only the individual who's lost it, and the staff who are doing the orchestrated takedown, remain. Without this measure, a hysterical girl can easily ignite mass hysteria, which can then become a riot, often adding more time to an inmate's sentence.

Ursula explained the necessity of takedowns to me. She was responding to how upset I was after seeing one for myself.

"For most of these girls," she said, speaking quietly, apart from everyone else, "life is a big bad storm. New girls arriving have no coping tools, nada. And they've never had boundaries. They only react, they never think out a response. Life is always blowing them away. We're trying to teach them here at ABG how to ride out those life-storms. But when they come here, all a girl knows is how to control, or be controlled. We're teaching them to cope, to change. Release the restraints of low self-esteem."

I smiled, listening to Ursula. She reminded me of someone.

Then I recalled my meditation teacher once talking about the benefits of "training one's inner demons." She had said, "That's the actual process of what a mindfulness practice really is: stilling the chattering monkey-mind."

"Oh yes," the teacher had explained, years before, "a common aphorism for this balancing act of living in the world and being able to accept disturbing events, is *walking on a razor's edge*. This comes from an ancient Sanskrit yogic sutra, a verse of scripture. As the allusion implies, becoming awake is when our consciousness becomes acutely aware. But sometimes that can put us on a precipice, the edge of life's slippery, sometimes deadly realities. The path to enlightenment is strewn with hazards. Only the strong of heart become sincere seekers. That's why we meditate. To still and fortify our confused minds we need to maintain equipoise, another word for serenity."

I focus on what Ursula is saying now. "But these girls are just trying to get through another crazy day in lockup! They're looking for ways to process the insane decisions they've made so far, the same thinking that led them to jail. Most don't have good role models. Lots have drugged-out or missing parents, or they've been raised by exhausted grandparents."

"Yes, I understand," I say, realizing how much more stressed these girls are than even I was, when I was a teenage alcoholic. At least my parents loved me. I had home-cooked meals every night. I had a warm bed and new shoes every school year. Many of these girls are angry because they didn't even have the bare necessities, like I did. They're addicted to being troublemakers, ten times more than suburban-me was, in my youth. On top of all their other problems, these girls at the academy, early on realized that acting out, even when destructive, and even though it got them into trouble—brought the attention they craved and never had at home.

I made a silent vow right then to help them learn how to turn their misery into a reasonably happy life. It worked for me, so I knew yoga and meditation would help them as well, through the hardships of even the worst days.

Ursula was nodding as she said, "The reason I prayed you up, teZa, is because I've always hoped to have less takedowns. And now that you're here, teaching the girls to tap the inner stuff, it's already happening. The pay-off of doing yoga while doing time, here in lockup, is learning how to let go of needing to control others, or letting others control us. They'll learn to trust the inner power that yoga harnesses."

Now it was my turn to nod in agreement. Ursula continued.

"I've told them a million times: We try any way we can to foster a state of amazement, by replacing old negative addictions with positive new ones. But you'll be showing them, even further, how to let go of addictions and develop mindfulness. Then, with their newly awakened perception, they'll choose better, starting with how to interact with others, which friends to pick, and what to eat. They'll have a chance to turn their anger and fear around. They can tap that place inside we all have, the loving compassionate side of ourselves. I'm so excited about the girls learning to be more thoughtful and respectful of themselves, above all else. And then, respectful of others."

I added, "Living thoughtfully far outweighs the turmoil of a pissed-off life. I was so relieved to learn that from my teachers."

Ursula agreed. "For these girls—hell-bent on either controlling or not being controlled—your being here is like having a goddess in our midst. I'm not trying to blow air up your ass, by the way."

We both laughed.

Ursula went on, "The worst thing for them is to continue to live half-asleep, that's where they are in active addiction. Denial and rage supersede any sense of awareness other than basic survival. With these repeat offenders, the smokescreen of self-righteousness is their only mirror."

I said with a chuckle: "For me, the choice was simple when it was laid out before me: cosmic consciousness or a woebegone Big Mac of self-pity. You're right, Ursula. It all boils down to control or be controlled, either by addictions or others—or learning to make our life a prayer. I found spiritual Truth when I opened my mind to what a good teacher can impart. You learn a lot, subliminally, just by being around a mentor. It's a lot easier when you have a role model."

"I'll say," Ursula said, looking over at the takedown which had quietly been going on for fifteen minutes. None of the four staff had moved. They remained on the floor, pressing their bodies around Nell, the Puerto Rican girl, who'd freaked after learning that her boyfriend on the Outs was seeing someone else.

"I look forward to the day," Ursula said, "when the girls learn there's another option besides seeking attention in such a negative way as violently acting out." She looked me in the eye before she said, "You have no idea how glad I am that you're here, showing the girls how to deal with their unmanageable emotions."

This is what a tree pose LOOKS like ...

... this is what it FEELS like!

CHAPTER 10

my beautiful girls

Because of budget restrictions, the academy's meals and snacks, all institutional fare, were shipped in from a local caterer, and eaten in two shifts in the large and windowless, echo-filled cafeteria. The order of each day was chaos-burgers, drama-casseroles, and hysterics-tacos: all favorites of teenage girls.

Even without a hurricane, tension is always off-the-wall-high in lockup. Gradually, my yoga girls learned to find peace in the midst of that mania.

Each class we have is always the same, week after week. First, we gather to sit in a circle and breathe deeply. New girls are taught how to release their *belly* with the in-breath (diaphragm breathing) and push it in with each out-breath. After a few rounds of quietly breathing, together we sing Om, the sound of All That Is. I explain Om to every new girl:

"Om has been called the *seed mantra*. A mantra is a word or phrase used to steady our busy minds, sometimes called the *monkey-mind*. When chanting Om we honor yoga as being about shifting gears, *going into another way of thinking* … that's why we start by sounding this sacred syllable. For centuries yogis have done the same. Om is how we honor the teachers, too, who've maintained the truths of yoga."

I always ask if there are any questions, and we spend a few minutes discussing each.

Next, we share the words printed on those small cards passed around when our circle first began, before our breathing exercise. Each girl speaks aloud the word printed on her card, and if she wishes, relates how it applies to her own life. If they don't want to share, they can pass. Usually, the word—whether it's *Peace, Love, Acceptance, Patience, Humility,* or any other of the positive affirmations on my handmade cards—sparks a discussion. This is a good way for the girls to get something off their chest, and I can offer them another point of view, a yogic one. The yogic approach, by the way, tells us that consciousness is within all, and every person is a spark of the sacred consciousness that's present throughout the Universe.

After our short opening, I say, "Okay! Let's rock 'n' roll. We'll stand to do our sun salutes." This is the warm-up period. We do the first salute super-slow, so any new girl can attain the moves with my instruction. Then we speed up for the next, and the next, and by the fifth everyone is loosey-goosey and ready for any pose I might throw their way.

These beautiful souls love the sensation of doing yoga. They tell me so, and they write about loving it in *Yoga Thoughts*, our class journal.

"I like the tree pose best. It makes me feel powerful to do something so hard!"

"The warrior is the bomb! Doing it makes me feel strong, like I'm not a victim anymore."

"I love the silence at the end of doing poses," one girl wrote, and many others agreed. "Yoga class is the only time I feel good inside."

"I love the altered state, the *high*, the different-than-normal that meditation is," another wrote. I explain often to my girls, "This is called *stilling the busy mind* and *tapping into supreme consciousness.* Meditation is the absence of thought."

Each new girl takes to it immediately. Why not? Meditation provides instant relief from the hardships of daily life, especially the stressful struggles of lockup. Meditation is an exercise of lightening life's burdens, mentally, that anyone can practice. Sometimes our so-called free state can be an internal prison of our own making.

The caretakers watch the improvement of the yoga girls, week by week. For Miss T's yoga girls, going to her class is like being in a secret society of happiness, complete with special names and impossible poses, and strange sounds like Om, but all adding up to an experience that's beyond anything any of them ever have known before. The rest of ABG's population, the non-yoga girls, are intrigued by yoga's mysteriousness, or skeptical, or downright mean to the yoga girls as they learn more each week about not letting others control the way they feel.

"See, girls," I repeat at every new class, "this is how we control our lives, by learning to control our breath. No one else breathes for us. We are the only ones in control of our lives, and how we breathe is proof-positive of this.

"In fact," I continue, "I would say here at the academy, the most important aspect of our yoga time together is to learn how powerful each of you is! No one has control over your spirit, even if they can keep your body in prison. If someone tries to control you, you can tell them—No Way!"

The girls are always astounded when I make it sound so simple. Sometimes I teasingly call our class *Spirit Controls Everything.* They laugh, thinking I'm joking. "But I'm not," I say with a jester's shrug. "When a person is in touch with their spirit, as yoga shows us, by using the focus of breath-control, and we learn to work with the energy that's needed to accomplish a pose—there's no control more powerful than that, which comes from within ourselves. And believe me, this is possible for everyone.

"Yoga teaches us that we have everything we need right inside," I remind my girls as they listen to their own breathing. "That's the only real control one ever has, over our own Self, our spirit Self."

Once in a while a new girl turns out to be a disser. This girl usually arrives in class as a jokester, but is quickly stunned by yoga's spontaneous power arising within, from the first deep intake of our breathing exercise. When one such gal experienced her first class, this former disser shouted, "Y'all need to try this!" to the other non-yoga troublemakers she passed when walking to her next class.

Some of the yoga girls are already mama to one, or in a few cases, two kids back home, cared for by their mother or grandmother. These girls, more eager to be *good* when they're released because of their children, are ultra-motivated to become committed yoginis. In our opening circle one young mother often says, "I'm going to be into this power-of-yoga stuff the same on the Outs as I am with my homie bros and sistahs."

Rebels arrive in class just like other types do. Desiree, a gang girl so tough even she doesn't know why she's trying yoga, finds she's mysteriously compelled to return, week after week because—she feels better. "As soon as I start breathing like you tell me to, I get high, get out of my head, and feel better," she wrote in our *Yoga Thoughts* journal.

The athlete or, more rarely, a dancer, comes because she's heard of yoga, knows it's "hip" and there are no other physical activities in lockup other than to stand around in the small grassy yard, surrounded by a plastic blackout fence. They want to continue training their body, as one put it. This girl is coordinated and graceful even though she's just like the others, suffering from terrifically low self-confidence, and an overdose of bad parenting.

Then there's the cutter. Shy, withdrawn, secretive, and nearly always a poet. One such girl is Alex, or *Durga, the peaceful goddess*, the spiritual name she chose for class. Soon to be released, she writes in the journal more than she speaks aloud. Privately, Durga shares her thoughts with me whenever I spend time with her, which I try to do a few minutes after each class. I hope to comfort her after reading her revealing first entry in Yoga Thoughts when she showed up in class, eight months earlier.

Durga is a sad, doe-eyed, quietly strong girl, who only has a week left to serve of her extended nine-month sentence. After that first class, Durga eagerly took to writing in the journal, in which I encouraged girls to express how they felt. She scribbled quickly as everyone was readying themselves to go to the next class.

When I later read Durga's note, addressed specifically to me, more than ever I realized why I was compelled to bring the calming effects of yoga to these disturbed girls. She'd written, "It's only when I'm in yoga class that I stop thinking about wanting to cut myself."

When I saw her next I said, "Thanks for sharing what you did last week."

Alex/Durga didn't say anything, and kept her gaze on the floor in front of her. I wondered if she was bashful, or just scared of life in general. I hoped she wasn't afraid of me. I so wanted to help this suffering girl. I'd never met a cutter before, not to my knowledge, but I'd heard of this common problem. My daughter Kara revealed to me later that one of her friends did it just so she "could feel something, anything!" Before she stopped communicating entirely with me, Kara related: "These girls would rather have pain and blood than not feel anything at all, like a zombie. That's what Beth told me, teZ. She cuts."

I'm speaking to Alex/Durga on the Thursday before Charley. "Are you excited about going home soon, Durga?"

She vehemently shakes her head, but now she's looking me straight in the eye. "I'm afraid of leaving the academy, Miss. Honestly, I'm more afraid than excited about having the freedom that I've been dreaming about for so long."

Cutting, or self-mutilation, is sadly more prevalent among female at-risk youth than average teenage girls. When I asked one girl—who had recently received a critical for cutting herself with a forgotten paperclip dropped by an administrator—why she did it, she answered with a shrug. Then she told me the same thing my daughter said earlier about her pal who cut: "It's the only way I can feel anything."

Alex/Durga went a little further in her explanation. After each class she'd write something to me, and I'd write back to her. Weekly, we had an ongoing, *private* correspondence in our Yoga Thoughts. Either she'd leave me a mysterious poem I couldn't decipher, or another snippet about herself. Then one day she wrote these words in our class journal:

"After living so long with so much abuse in my family, I learned to shut it out. To not feel anything. That's how I discovered that cutting myself, watching the blood, at least gave me *some* feeling. But when I do yoga I feel this awesome deep connection *inside* that I've never had before. I don't want to cut myself ever again. I'm going to do yoga when I'm on the Outs and now I can't wait!!"

I was excited to read this several weeks ago. Yet now I'm feeling Alex's apprehension when she tells me how scared she is to go home. I'll relate this news to Ursula later, and, sure enough, true to Ursula's commitment to help her girls both in prison and on the Outs, she'll arrange for Alex to live in a halfway house, instead of going back to an abusive home. Alex's mother is an alcoholic, her older teen brother has tried to get sexual with her, and Alex's father isn't anywhere in the picture. No one knows where he is.

For the remainder of her time at the academy I encourage Alex/Durga to continue with her simple yoga practice of five sun salutes, a headstand, and at least a few minutes of meditation, which she does in her room each evening. "You'll keep the connection alive with these simple rituals, Durga," I assure her.

Seeing her smile is like discovering the pot of gold at the end of the rainbow for me. A path leading from her unmanageable pain of before, is now heading toward my open heart. I hear her pain. I recognize her need for love. Her eyes shine with gratitude as they look deeply into mine, lessening the pain of losing my own daughter's love. I need a hug like I figure Alex does as well. I break all the rules right then, and encircle my arms around her newly awakened self.

Durga and I stand a moment, enjoying each other's closeness as the other girls noisily line up under the supervision of Mr. Lawrence, ready to go single-file to their next class. She and I don't touch after our quick embrace, it's frowned on in lockup. We stand regarding each other silently, as close as possible when physical contact between anyone isn't allowed.

CHAPTER 11

an easy way to change

At the back of the yoga class sits Mr. Lawrence, listening to his crackling walkie-talkie. I sigh in frustration at the man's indifference and focus on my circle of girls. After our opening breath work and yogic sharing, we begin the warm-up sun salutes. I put on soothing yoga music from the tape recorder I bring each week (it's before CDs, remember).

"As we move, keep focused on where I tell you to put your limbs—while remaining connected to your breath," I say. "Remember, that to still ourselves, especially when we're feeling anxious, worried, upset or unhappy, we begin with being conscious of our breath—even when doing something challenging like a sun salute."

All around us the air buzzes with the excitement of our shared emotion.

"Breathe consciously, stay in tune," I encourage, "stretch those arms out and overhead, that's great! Feel the air come in and out of your lungs in long steady breaths, bend your knees and fall forward, like a rag doll. That's right! Now just stay here and listen to your breath for a few rounds as your lower back unloosens its tension."

Automatically, every girl's conscious attention becomes sharper. She relaxes with the diversion of following the instructions for belly-breathing. I try to make the step-by-step lessons as entertaining as a radio talk show, filled with jokes, nothing serious. More engaging that way. Helpful to still minds when a teacher's voice leads to fragrant meadows of imaginary delights, a good place to be instead of jail.

At the present moment the thought-*koan* I offer my yoga girls on this Thursday, before Charley's due to ravage Florida, goes something like this:

"Relax in rag doll, and listen to your breath.

"Just as we of the delicate species known as humans must breathe, so too our glorious garden planet breathes as well. Our lives mirror what the Earth experiences. Each human is a microcosm of the macrocosm. It's the breath—whether of our lungs or of the Earth's winds that circle the globe—that unites everything."

At the start of Thursday's class we discussed Hurricane Charley, which was going to give us a windier day than usual, but nobody had a clue if it would hit, or how devastating it might be. We'd already been through Hurricane Alex, then pipsqueak Bonnie. And now—just another annoying bad-weather day. That's what we are thinking on Thursday. The girls don't seem too concerned about any storm but those raging in their own lives. In our opening circle they wanted to talk of more urgent issues than "dumb old hurricanes."

"I miss my boyfriend," Yolanda says.

"I'm happy today," one girl pipes up.

"I've lost weight," Eternia chimes in.

"I feel my heart opening so wide when doing yoga with you, Miss T," Melissa claims.

"I'm worried 'bout my mamma, she's sick," Theresa murmurs dejectedly.

Our opening circle is a time of sharing and making intentions. Again the cards I pass around help the girls focus.

"I got Forgiveness today," MaryAnn says. "Doing yoga has helped me forgive my parents for not being there for me. They did their best."

I look outside the window to see a huge semi speeding down the main drag in the one-stoplight town of Bowling Green. I smile, flashing on what this place must look like to the truck driver: just a blur on his gluey-with-guts windshield, here in the *lovebug* capital of the world, central Florida. I listen to Leticia.

"I miss my baby daughter," she says. "But I know I'll be a better mom now when I'm on the Outs."

It feels good to me, coming to this place of sorrow to offer tools that help them. I'm wondering why the girls don't seem more concerned about the hurricane approaching us. The news announcer said this morning, "This could be the worst multiple hurricane season in Florida's history." In the far Atlantic, over by Africa, the newscaster said, other hurricanes were brewing behind this one, Charley.

After each of the twelve girls in our circle has shared her thoughts or passed, and before we begin our sun salutes, I offer them what I've been thinking on the long drive here.

"Bad weather can be likened to Earth's breath becoming congested," I said. "Much like when we get a cold, or a bad cough. In a hurricane, tornado, or a tsunami, and earthquakes, too, Nature gets swept away with its own power. We all know about naturally occurring disasters. The insurance world calls these, *Acts of God*. Of course, people are in danger whenever the weather gets fierce, when the planet's breath gets congested."

I have the girls' attention now.

"So when threats come, weather-wise or by people—first, make sure you're safe. Which you are here, in this fort of a building. Want to guess what you do next?"

Omkara, one of my regulars who's come to yoga for months, raises her hand. "Follow our breath, right?"

"Right, Omkara. You don't want to panic when bad things start to happen. As long as you know you're safe, and you don't have to find shelter, the best thing to do, no matter how many people start to lose it around you—is to stay in the calm within your own inner Being, and follow your breath."

The girls are listening intently to me and to their peers in our opening circle. They don't seem to realize how serious this hurricane can be. As I encourage the girls to discuss whatever is on their minds, the concerns of any teenager—misunderstandings, disappointments—I continue to think about the bigger picture outside these walls of lockup. As we speak, the fury, the erratic path of a monster storm is rampaging five-hundred miles away, heading for Cuba, but raging right toward Florida also.

Good, I think, the girls understand calm. But tomorrow? Now's the time to prepare them. They've never experienced a hurricane's eye, as I have.

I then speak of the peace within we get from doing yoga, how it's analogous to the peace within the eye of every hurricane.

Our circle grows quiet. I continue.

"People can prepare for hurricanes way ahead of time. Shelter, food, and other necessities have to be readied. Like fragile insects, some of us shudder and run to hide in our little burrows, pretending to be safe even when we don't feel we are.

"The birth of a hurricane is a balancing act that gives as well as takes. Nourishing breath and life-giving waters combine in a hurricane, to create incredible power. Humans can do nothing to stop the fury of a rampaging cyclone of wind, a volcanic eruption, a wall of water. All we can do after finding safe shelter—is find our inner place of rest.

"So tomorrow, girls—we don't know what's going to happen. Nobody does. You have the right to know the truth, though, how dangerous it is to even be *near* the eye of a hurricane. Regardless of what tomorrow brings, I want you to know that you will be absolutely safe. *Nothing* can affect this strong building. Ms. Ursula knows this, and I know it, so don't let anyone convince you otherwise. Today, we're practicing how to feel just as safe inside your own Beingness, as you are inside this building. And if ABG does get a direct hit from Charley's eye, it'll be scarier than you can imagine.

"So it's important to be aware of this ahead of time, girls. Don't waste energy panicking or giving in to worry. Even if all the other girls surrounding you are losing it, you yoga girls can overcome anything, not just when facing Charley, but for any storm that strides too close to your life. You know, more than any of the other girls here—nothing can hurt you, no circumstance, no other person, nothing!—when you stay safe in your inner *'I'*."

I look around the circle. The girls are peaceful and quiet. What I'm sharing with them is near and dear. I take a deep breath and go one step further.

"My journey to inner peace has been the saving grace of my life," I say. "It was through practicing yoga that I found my own center within."

I take a deep breath and stretch my spine, asking and receiving direction from the inner Source, on how to present this most-important topic to my girls.

"A hurricane," I continue, "has a long ferocious front wall of destruction, then mere minutes within its calm eye, before the wind gets crazy again coming from the reverse direction. Unlike an insane hurricane, though, any person can choose to stay safely, deeply in the center of their own life-storm all the time—if they want."

Every girl is stone-still. Listening. No one's in a rush to shift the mood.

"That place within us—the *'I'* of a person's inner Self—offers shelter from every storm we must pass through."

I look around the circle and see a few girls rocking in quiet assurance, while others remain still. All want to understand. They have grown to trust me. I have been a steady presence at the academy, and no one has ever heard a lie come from me. The girls know I wouldn't deceive them about a deadly storm that's headed our way.

I continue. "The fierce trials of life that try to blow us away, appear every now and then. But there's a safe harbor within every center of conflict, if we choose to trust it. We don't have to get caught up in the whirling madness of crazy emotions, or crazy hurricanes. That safe harbor within is a state of mind that anyone can access. It's on the inside of us, not on the outside. Not even when you're on the Outs. No person, no lover, no amount of money, fame or things will ever give you this inner peace I'm talking about, except when you find that place within your own Self."

We've talked about this idea of inner peace a lot in yoga class. The regulars have lots of practice experiencing it because we always end each class with a period of quiet relaxation, called *savasana*, or the aware-corpse pose. But the newer girls, especially Tara, have not considered this concept of inner peace, never having had much chance to practice being still before. The idea that there's peace at the core of every person's Beingness has never entered a new girl's mind, ever. One by one, the regulars get it. Tara got it. The concept of a sanctuary, within. Soon everyone is smiling, laughing, lapping up this truth like hungry kittens given warm milk.

I go on. "To rest forever in the center—the eye of a hurricane—would, of course, be the safest way to go through any storm. But that's impossible with a real hurricane. Because a storm travels, and a storm's amorphous eye charges along with it. So, we poor humans have to take on the front plus the back assault of each hurricane we encounter. We can't stay in its eye, we only get to be in it when it travels over us.

"However, in life-storms, the emotional challenges we all go through—it is totally possible to stay in one's own center. This place, is no place. It's found when we choose to foster a spiritual life. It's the sacred space we find in each empowerment class. And anytime we remember to go within, no matter what's going on outside, we can find in that spiritual center of our own life—our inner *'I'* —the reward of inner peace. Choosing to stay in our own inner *'I'* is every person's birthright."

I fall silent now.

"Wow," Shay whispers. ShakespearesDelight is one of the few regulars who's never asked for a yoga name.

"Yeah, I'll say. Wow," I agree and nod my head. The other girls are silently absorbing this convincing concept I've put forth, here and many other times. But today, I'm speaking more urgently, due to Charley's expected arrival. Deep inside, the confirmed yoga girls know it's true. They've already experienced that center. To them individually and as a class, I've spoken of this truth again and again.

"It may be impossible to stay forever in the middle of a hurricane's eye, but with practice, it's possible to reside in one's own inner *'I'* most of the time. That's called staying in our Big Heart. It's also called being true to our Self, our higher Self, not the lower self that's prone to emotional upsets, being addicted, feeling *the victim*. It's a matter of choosing to detach from the pain of bad feelings."

I take a deep breath and let my head sink into the compassionate cave of my heart.

Looking at all the attentive faces in our circle, I say: "We practice staying in our *'I'* by following our breath, over and again, until the habit of detaching from negatives, sticks. Then—nothing can wound our strong spirits, ever again."

CHAPTER 12

how on earth?

Once, long before Charley's drama descended, I addressed a new girl who appeared in class that day.

"Doing yoga will demonstrate for you, Dana, that you have within yourself the power to change. You don't need a teacher, book, or any other person to tell you anything—if, the big *IF*—you know how to tap that core part of your self. You just decide to trust, go inside to your quiet inner *'I'*... and stay there. And guess what? You'll feel safe.

"Then, when we practice our *asanas*, the poses, we can go even further within, exploring our inner selves. We go deeper into a physical pose as well as its spiritual understanding. We achieve peace by focusing on our breath. Otherwise the pose can't be achieved. Your own body shows you the benefit of focusing within. With steadiness, our eyes gaze on a single spot. We learn to look within, this way as well; not just on outside stuff that distracts us. First we'll learn a simple pose. Then we'll go deeper into it, and gradually we begin to—anytime, anyplace—access the incredible power that's our own being, and own it, this inner *'I'*."

"I want that!" Dana exclaims.

"Good," I cheer. "Because all you have to do is want this experience, and it is yours! All you have to do"—I look around at the seasoned yoga girls, who have been nodding along—"is practice the focusing exercises you're learning here."

"I *really* want it," Dana exclaims. The girl next to her, Lakendra, high-fives Dana. Everyone then bursts out laughing. There's so much joy in the room, we're all so glad to be free from head-trips, others' control, anger, depression, or any other demons that have tried to possess us. With heads nodding, eleven girls are telling Dana how they each felt the same during their first yoga class.

"We all want it," Vonda mock-scolds. "That's why we're here, you fool."

Dana looks at me with stunned excitement. She's ready.

I stand. "Let's be girl-mountains now, in *tadasana*, the mountain pose. This is how we start. Then we'll do our sun salutes."

I align myself and say to the girls who are standing in a circle around me, "No bent arms or slouching on one leg. Remember, we're not tea cups with handles or spouts sticking out," I tease. "We're statuesque, strong girl-mountains." I look around. "Excellent mountains! Remember to keep your gaze steady in front of you, attuned to one point. That's called the *drishti*, our focus. A little Buddha smile's helpful, thank you! However steady your eyes are, that's the secret of a successful pose."

Everyone smoothly gets into the standing pose—stretching spines, elongating necks, looking straight ahead—creating their own beautiful mountain song with their body, their still limbs and sky-high posture. I look around our circle and think, "It's true: we're an unbroken chain, a mountain range of gorgeous females, young and old, working to better ourselves."

The *tea cup* thing is a joke, good for eliciting laughs whenever a girl forgets and slouches; old habits die hard. With one arm sticking out like a spout, the other on a swaying hip handle, I sing the kid-song of looking like *a tea cup*. Just like when I tease the occasional germ-phobic resident whose bare feet are covered by the academy's mandatory but slippery polyester socks. I will scowl and say, "Only yoga sissies wear those dangerous things in my class! They make it impossible to grip those gorgeous toes of yours on this magnificent carpet. You'll never be balanced. I need you to sign a release before you slip, if you insist."

These girls love to be cajoled and kidded. The sock-fanatics grunt and usually take theirs off, to the others' cheers. No one wants an injury. No one wants to be called a sissy, either. We all want to feel safe, even in lockup. No one was ever injured in my class, and I brought anyone who asked right up into a full, *aha*-moment headstand, always, in their first attempt. Easy, with proper instructions. And no socks.

Dana says, "Miss T, I wants to be upside down!" With my assistance, she achieves the alignment, and up she goes without so much as a grunt. Then five other girls get up on their own while I help some newer girls who are ready to try this challenging pose.

"You look beautiful, girls. Powerful. Full of Power, yeah! Remember, any mindful practice like yoga combines mental, physical and spiritual disciplines. What we're doing is learning all the tools you'll ever need to empower your life."

If a person repeatedly practices only *hatha yoga*—the physical part, which has many other expressions besides just poses—they inevitably start to feel empowered in all other aspects of life: the mental, the emotional, the spiritual. Yoga and other mindfulness, meditative, core-strengthening modalities (Pilates, the martial arts, tai chi) offer people the ability to be consciously in the center of calm that lies within us all. The variety of life-storms—be they emotional, ethical, political, religious, social, and most especially, spiritual turmoil—can go on ad infinitum. There are many iterations of upheaval that manifest in humanity.

Dana asks for a name and Kali, who's in charge of the list, has suggested she choose *Ananda*. "It means *filled with bliss*," Kali tells Dana, a pale waif who looks totally opposite from the stereotypical teenager-in-trouble. With her porcelain-clear skin, dark blond hip-style hair, and sparkling hazel eyes behind black glasses, she openly shares at our opening circle: "It's easy to be carried away by wants ... by drugs ... by sex."

"I know what you mean," I answer Dana, now Ananda during class. No one's allowed to use their yoga names outside our group because it would signify separation from the rest of the population, and too closely resembles the use of gang names.

"I'm just like you all," I say, and notice the regulars' head-nods. They may be tired of the repetition, but each new girl needs to hear it from me. "Only I wasn't caught as young as you were." This is how I establish equality, unity and solidarity in our class.

"What? You been in prison, Miss T!" Dana/Ananda shouts, her voice super-charged with its high-voltage.

"We know," the rest clamor in fun, "but tell us again!" The girls never tire of hearing about the "old me" ... not the one who's a wife and mother and respected community member. Juicy details I'm reluctant to share with others, but know it's important for them to realize: I'm the same as they are. Kali rubs her face, having heard this before. For the moment I focus on Ananda.

I laugh. "Sure. I'm just like each of you, but I wasn't given the opportunity to change so early in life, like you girls have." They all sit perfectly still, a little uneasy imagining their together-looking guide, once a criminal like them. To their eyes, I appear to be just like Ursula, the respectable shrink who runs this show, showing up each week in my tight yoga duds to spend time doing pretzel-poses with them. Until they hear it from me personally, it's impossible for them to believe I could have ever been remotely like them. But I keep reminding them, because it's healing to feel equal.

I've given enough information for that day. "Come on, let's do some yoga!" I insist. "Enough discussion. Any questions? Okay, so we'll sit on the floor and chant *Om* three times to shift gears from *normal* to *yoga*-mind. Ready to raise our consciousness, girls? Let's close our eyes, breathe a few rounds, and connect to our inner power, which is ever-abundant. And then we'll do some kick-butt *asanas*, poses to put our living temples, our bodies, into the best shape possible. Ready?"

At other times in other classes, I've told my yoga girls more. How life woke me up one day and, instead of wanting to die, I started to laugh at my self-centered foolishness. Gradually, I learned about the Bigger, Better-me, the one that's capitalized—the Self that's within us all. The capital S—Self—is the spiritual center of our lives, as I share often; whereas the small-letter self, is our physical *shell*, or temple, as I prefer to call our body. Which, as we all know, can get filled to the brim with emotional *stuff.*

As Hurricane Charley roars his way toward us in central Florida that Thursday with Dana/Ananda in attendance, I continue sharing how to be more thoughtful, steady, balanced, strong, and empowered as we achieve one pose after another, until we've done many asanas. Five of the girls have been coming regularly and I let them think they can practically run the class by themselves. I ask one, then another, to lead us with instructions as I call out the next pose after we've warmed up with five sun salutes. In turn, we wrap our limbs into rabbit, crow, camel poses, each girl I ask leading the others to the best of her ability. Ananda is all in, and does amazingly well for a first-timer.

I consider the class before me. Many of these girls' lives have already changed drastically just by practicing yoga for one hour a week. Some write in *Yoga Thoughts* that they practice in between our time in class together, like Shanti/Carol who tells me she practices each morning and evening in her room. Some tell me they strike a pose wherever they can for the rest of ABG—especially the non-yoga girls—to see and wonder about.

I glance over to the shadows of the common room where we are doing yoga doing time. The academy's community altar is there in its out-of-the-way corner of the big common room. I have often added something special to it, like the time I brought one of my heart-shaped rocks. "This signifies my love for you, all of you who come to class, and the girls who don't," I explained. We start our routine: the sharing circle, our various poses. Without mats or mirrors, accompanied by the sweet sound of a mellow chant playing continuously, the mood is one of repose and joy.

Without a doubt the favorite part of class for all—regular yoga girls and first-timers alike—is at the end of class when we sink into relaxing *savasana*, the bliss-guided meditation I offer. My gentle words lead them to a stillness within, followed by a brief time of silence. Everyone considers this the icing on our class-cake we've been baking together. The session has been challenging because all the girls are out of shape. Being in lockup has turned even the most athletic of them into jellied couch potatoes. Our final moment of tranquility feels like gold to everyone. How sad, I often think, without this weekly yoga class, they'd have absolutely no physical activity other than walking aimlessly.

CHAPTER 13

resistance is human

The undeniable truth, however, is that most girls who end up in lockup are not interested in changing. Less than half the population, way less, gravitated into my class at one time or another "to check it out." Some came once and never again. One new girl got freaked out when I started off (and I'll never do it again, believe me) going into the "courage-feeling Lion Pose," as I call it, that day ages before Charley.

When Jasmine saw me and eleven others kneeling with hands extended on our knees, right after Om-ing (strange enough for any newbie) then cross our eyes, and fully thrust out our tongues while making a forceful *ROAR* like a pissed-off lion—she jumped up and screamed, "You guys are crazy! Let me outta here!" and ran for the exit, never to return. Sure, I was sad I'd lost her. Right then I resolved to never start any class with this formidable pose, certain to frighten the daylights out of anyone the least bit fearful.

Some days only five or six girls showed up. Stress rules in lockup. Despite having practiced our yogic "tools," many girls succumbed to depression, anger, their monthly ennui, and the constant drama of romance. Ursula explained the way it was on that very first visit of mine. "In prison reform we say, Everyone's gay for the stay. Everyone, hetero or gay, tries to have sex with one another."

The ones who showed up in my class each week were a rare species among incarcerated youth. Many others scoffed openly at "that nonsense," and during free-time spat on the ground (outside) when either yoga or my name was mentioned. They'd harrumph and slump away when inside, and make it plain they weren't ready to embrace a change in their anti-health, self-pitying ways. Only those girls who had open hearts and minds—those not yet jaded, but ready and brave enough for something new—had a chance to make real progress away from their anger-fueled false perceptions. Girls who embraced change were the ones who kept showing up each week. They were the ones who didn't mind working hard to earn the reward of inner peace; the ones who got to enjoy the icing on the yoga-cake, the deep rejuvenation of meditation.

Kali was eager to try yoga. She was one of only ten girls who volunteered to attend the first class after the demonstration I gave for the whole assembly in the crowded common room, the one with the subtly placed, protected altar in a far-off corner. I had prepared a Xeroxed handout with sketches I drew of the several easy poses we would be doing that day, along with words of encouragement on how yoga not only builds strong bodies but strong minds and a shiny spirit.

Earlier, Ursula informed me that the greater percentage of girls at the facility had landed there because of unhealthy family environments. "Most," she said, "have been abused, either physically or mentally." She then warned me that a lot of the girls didn't like to be touched, "even in a natural, affectionate manner. It's just something we try not to do, the staff I mean." She then asked me not to hug anyone—"without first getting their permission." I agreed to respect this request even though it went against my grain, having a flexible, easy-going nature like most yoga folks. "Touch the girls only when absolutely necessary," Ursula suggested, a guideline antithetical to the *adjusting-method* used by many yoga teachers.

The day came, very quickly I'm afraid, when I inevitably forgot and adjusted one of my aspiring yoginis. Katy, who had chosen her new yoga name of Kali, the fierce *defender of righteousness*, was in a difficult position, bent over sidewise in the triangle pose, in class that day. When I saw her twisted, contorted form, naturally I forgot, and lightly touched her crooked hip to help re-align her into the proper position.

Kali jumped up and backed off as if bitten by a snake at the tender touch of my fingertips. Bouncing upright like a rubber band, Kali yelped like a whipped dog, her eyes blazing with fury, her mouth pulled tight into a terrified grimace. She stood apart from me and the rest of the group, fists raised, ready to rumble. I too, jumped back a step, frightened for the first time since wanting to teach these roughneck girls. Kali had been to all four of the previous classes we'd had. She was a big hefty white gal, already a mom of a two-year-old. She lowered her fists to her sides, breathing hard, glancing between me and the other girls, ready to show everybody *who* was in charge of *her* life. Quickly, I realized my mistake.

"I'm so sorry," I stammered. "I forgot, Katy, I mean, Kali. I should have asked your permission first. It won't happen again, I promise."

She immediately relaxed. "Okay, then." She shape-shifted again, turning to snicker with her friends who'd witnessed my apology. These girls needed as much respect as they could get, as anyone does, to discover true Self-respect.

She only relaxed after I offered additional reassurance, explaining my intention was only to adjust her pose, something considered standard operating procedure for teachers. "It's usual to manually adjust students; but certainly, it's optional," I added.

I told all the girls that from then on, "I'll be more careful and only touch you after getting your permission." Murmurs of approval rose up, smiles returned, attitudes relaxed. I asserted my willingness to accommodate my students, and they responded with genuine interest about our yogic work together. I let go of what works on the Outs in a *normal* yoga class, and received respect and kindness in return.

In order to guide a student into attaining the knowledge to make progress when learning something new, being flexible is the best, besides the yogic way. Yoga is an ancient and complex science. Detailed instructions help one to understand its depths, whether about a pose, or the philosophy of yoga. Like, how a person spontaneously experiences the awakening of higher consciousness. This happens through the opening of energy centers known as *chakras*. Doing the poses causes the *opening* of these energy centers to happen, when a person regularly practices.

I didn't think it relevant to explain to the girls at ABG yoga's more esoteric concepts, like a person's Kundalini awakening, which often happens to regular yoga practitioners. But I certainly did answer any question when they came up during our opening circle's discussion.

Only when Kali agreed to re-join the group, did I relax. This was a test for all of us. The other girls looked on, curious to see how their new yoga teacher would handle confrontation. Kali/Katy was satisfied my touch had been inadvertent. Still, I saw Mr. Lawrence rise from his standard slouch in the back of the room when Katy started screeching her objection. It was a tense moment. I knew Lawrence would be trigger-quick on the radio if there was any indication of the need for a takedown. But Kali was appeased by my apology. I watched Lawrence sit down, return to his usual slouch, and put the walkie-talkie back to his ear.

We went on with our poses. But I could tell the girls were more confident now that I, the tall, oddly muscular woman who came to do yoga with them each week, was really there to help them. I could tell this confrontation made a dent in their resistance. And me—well, I learned just how damaged these *ordinary-looking* captured juvie offenders really were.

Not much later, 17-year-old Kali/Katy became infamous among her peers in the teen-slammer for *absconding,* as the girls snidely called running away. It happened when she was awarded a much-coveted weekend-home pass, only to ruin it, and her good record, by going on a drug-and-sex binge, not seeing her baby the whole time she was off with her crazy druggy boyfriend, a biker. Up to that point, Kati had never missed a single yoga class the entire time she was a resident. Ursula asked Katy when she was returned to the academy in handcuffs, with six-months added to her already lengthy sentence (she'd been there since she was sixteen), why she did it. The girl only shrugged.

But later, she fessed up in our opening circle in yoga class, "How can life possibly be interesting without sex and drugs, rap and hip-hop?" Kali wailed, "I just needed a break!"

"Praise be Tupac!" a dark-haired girl called French Fry, a black girl with haunted eyes, cried out in solidarity with this show of rebellion.

"Yah mohn, Tupac! our baby Panther, martyr-man," Sha'Ron, another girl of color who coined her creative yoga name, *Durganeesha,* shouted in a jubilant sing-song, raising her right fist high in salute to the slain thug life rapper.

Others giggled and nodded. I took a deep breath and thought, "Okay, this is an opportunity here." For what, I never knew till I plunged in. No other girl but Kali had dared be "so bad" as to run away during her sentence. Before her misadventure, Kali/Katy was the ideal yoga girl in lockup. The academy's triple-locks and barbwire fences prevented anyone from busting out. Disappearing on a home pass was almost unthinkable to these desperate-to-be-free girls—but Kali did it.

Life for girls at ABG was, and for some always will be—getting laid, getting high, and acting out. They think being fucked-up is fun, or, at least, before lockup they did. Before getting caught they *wanted* to get fucked-up on anything, anyone, anyhow, on purpose, in any way, shape or form. Some of them still think that being behind wire fences and locked doors is just a minor imposition to the continuation of their game. Agitation, rough talk, dissin' each other, and sexual superiority were the measures of self-worth in these girls' limited perspectives. Disruption and unease are the only kind of existence they've ever known. Getting calm, discovering their own spiritual center, these words introduced to them in Miss T's yoga class, at first seemed ... well, "boring and dumb," as Kali now explained in her post-runaway group discussion. I nodded. I knew that to new girls first coming to yoga, *spiritual* was an *unknown* to them.

"I know I let you down, Miss T," Kali said.

"You didn't let me down, not at all. If anything, you let yourself down."

"I know. But I like sex best of all," Kali smugly admitted. The other girls high-fived each other with "Yessssses" going around our circle like a giant serpent awakened, one that only loves the verb-noun, Sex.

"But," Kali shouts above the ruckus, "I know I was stupid. Now I have to wait so much longer to be with my baby and my man."

I said, "Kali, we all make mistakes. Now we can get to work, and you can learn to choose better while you're still here! Think of that, instead of what you're missing."

"Like what?"

"Like all those poses you say you want to learn. And y'know, girls, being a yoga teacher on the Outs is something you might all want to consider. Especially you, Kali. You're so good at doing the poses. Yoga's become popular now, thanks to Madonna and Sting and every style-ista under the sun; plus, teaching yoga is a good job opportunity. And way more healthy than, say, working in a bar."

Kali's eyes lit up. "Me? A yoga teacher? Like you?"

"Sure, why not? You're a natural. You've loved doing the poses and meditation in class for a year and a half now. You're practically my assistant. Matter of fact, why don't you lead us today? I think that's a good way of welcoming our vagabond back, don't you, girls?" I asked the others, looking at eleven astonished sets of eyes.

Kali beamed such happiness as she led us in the opening sun salutes. Then I asked a different regular to guide us as we went into warrior poses, a half-moon, an eagle, and on to the floor poses of bridge, head-to-knee, and the girls' giggly-favorite asana, Buddha baby, when we hold our big toes and rock sideways on our lower back.

As we slipped into the quiet of meditation, lying relaxed and at ease on the carpet, facecloths over the eyes, I noticed the girls instantly dropping into that deep relaxed state, when thoughts are turned off. For these few minutes, they could explore the safe interior place where calm and peace and complete freedom were theirs.

mind-body-spirit is what we really are

CHAPTER 14

freedom is an inside job

On Friday the 13th, Charley is raging towards the academy. Its hundred-mile-wide expanse creeps forward like a spiraling fury at only a few miles an hour, upturning and devouring everything in its path.

At Bowling Green, the upset girls are told by Miss Estelle, "Soon we be gathering all together. Even if that ol' Mister Charley eye decides to come right at us—we be safe like he be a big ol' pussycat. Don't you worry none, girls."

Yesterday's class ended like every other one, with savasana. In a slow and quiet voice, I led them into meditation.

"After fortifying our physical side, our body, now we'll release from that part of ourselves and explore our deeper, spiritual side.

"Mind-body-spirit is what we really are, not just the outside we can *see*. Deep inside, we'll touch who you *really* are. Rest here, and learn to *Be* with your true Self, the deeper one within you. The part of *you* that has a connection with an unlimited, unexplainable energy. It's totally magical. You have the same power—this energy within you, that in yoga is called *the Kundalini* energy—it's the same power within everything. It's our common denominator. Some people call it God within. Others call it Nature. Some give it names like the Force, as in the *Star Wars* movies. Some call it simply, the Source of All.

This God-energy is a part of you and you're part of It. That's what we're exploring now. Follow your breath in, deeply; follow your breath out, long."

Kali said it like it is. "I like sex best." I never directly addressed the sex-thing in our opening circle, because that would not have been appropriate; but I'll share my thoughts about some of the insights I got from teaching my girls.

People everywhere have as strong a sexual urge as the dominant life force that throbs within all of us. An adolescent's sex urge arises at the same time as questions about their existence does, and these are spiritual questions. So which gets fostered, sex or spirit? The challenge for mindful, compassionate people is to not let either rule our lives. Balancing sex and spirit, mind and body, has a big payoff. Balance is the price tag for health and happiness. Discovering how to balance, ahhh, that's the challenge of human existence.

Similar conflicts to what the entire world faces appear in microcosm in any community of gathered humans. At Miss Ursula's academy for *Wayward Girls*, and other detention facilities, sexual competition and hostilities occur in this forced internment. Gay for the stay is the accepted standard—like Ursula quoted to me the correctional workers' stance—no matter what an inmate's natural sexual orientation may be.

To an individual, overpopulation and stress trigger odd, otherwise uncharacteristic behavior. I've been told by the academy's staff that the biggest problem by far, in any community of locked-up girls aged twelve to eighteen, is sexual misconduct.

Ursula told me straight when I first arrived. Sexual games at ABG were clandestine and competitive. Not surprising at all, considering the population was isolated from any competing partners, male or female. Plus they were lonely, homesick, and crowded together with no respite from the constants of anxiety-driven noise and high-pitched aggravation and aggression. Fights happened way more than chats. Everyone accepted it: even hetero girls became gay *just* for the stay.

There was no privacy whatsoever, except when the toilet door was closed. Room checks at night to guard against sexual activity couldn't stop the bed-sharing in a two-girl room. When those doors closed, girls invented sexual intrigue, figuring out ways to keep their pairing-off, switching, drama-games going, even though bed-checks were regular throughout the night. At this age, youth rage with sexual energy anyway, but the restriction of having no freedom only adds to a teenager's need for sexual release of any sort. Covert goes with the scene in jails and lockup.

In yoga the sexual energy is described as happening coincidingly with the awakening of the spiritual yearning and wondering, called *Kundalini Shakti.* A tremendous upsurge of energy (shakti) arises in an individual when the spiritual (Kundalini) center of a person has been awakened, or *vice versa.* The ecstasy that naturally happens when a person lets awakened consciousness into their life, is something every lover of a person, or of God enjoys, from the first teenage crush, or a fundamental religious person's afterlife beliefs, to the spiritual seeker's pursuit of Oneness. Many people never experience the spiritual awakening because if it's not fostered it quickly goes back to its inner, still-sleeping state and lies dormant again—if the Kundalini isn't nurtured after its spontaneous awakening in adolescence. It's precisely then, in the teens, that a young person's newly awakened sexual life takes off, explodes— becoming uncontrollable—if their spirit is not nurtured. Exactly what happened to all the girls at ABG.

(As an aside, I also taught adolescent boys in lockup, but only breath work and meditation, never yoga poses. Three of us meditators would visit different detention centers. Others before us, who'd brought spiritual practices to inmates, had found that males are best to teach other males the physical poses of hatha yoga. Experience has it that all those butt-up-in-air poses only cause trouble with male libidos if a female instructs them. Any prisoner, male or female, experiences great relief the instant they're shown how to properly breathe, and how to sit in the stillness of meditation. This was my focus in teaching boys in lockup.)

Sometimes though, later in life and usually after a traumatic event—the loss of a loved one, or some other catalyzing catastrophe—one can again experience the awakening of their Kundalini—this time spontaneously. In a flash, an instant, even. All it takes is to be caught in the middle of a life-storm—or a hurricane—or to meet someone special whose vibration resonates with theirs. Sometimes going through a traumatic event may be the only thing that shakes up a person's set ways, the doors of their inner perceptions being flung open—by force. The awakening can happen at any time in life, but the first awakening happens to all of us as young teens.

This yearning *to know the secret of life* appears through natural occurrences, coinciding with the time when a youth starts to ask questions such as, *Who am I?* and *Why am I here?* This yearning desire is the awakened Kundalini. This desire can, if not properly directed into creative or spiritual outlets, become a raging compulsion to explore the mysteries of sex, the corresponding energy, along with being creative and knowing Spirit, that overwhelms and captivates many humans.

The creative energies of sexual and spiritual yearnings arise from the same energy source. This occurrence is described in yogic scriptures as the opening, or activating of second chakra energy. A *chakra* means a *wheel* of energy (consciousness) that lies dormant within all people, waiting to be *awakened*. The ancients described the seven chakras in detail to help explain the ever-elevating, potential consciousness that all humans have within us.

The activating of creative consciousness happens right after a person's first chakra, of basic survival instincts, has been activated. Next, the second chakra activates. The awakening of creative energy can be of a sexual (the pro-*creation* of our species), artistic (creativity in all forms), and/or spiritual-yearning (the big questions of adolescence: Who Am I? What is Existence?).

The nature of creativity is as vast as, well, all of Creation. The creative urge has an ever-expanding potentiality and takes on unlimited forms. How absolutely perfect to ensure our species procreates that the creative urge arises right after the staying-alive instinct is sufficiently functioning.

When every child arrives at the door of puberty, their second chakra's creative urge kicks in, right on evolutionary schedule.

We all know about the raging hormones that plague every teenager. And most know how sexual and spiritual energies are interlinked. Just look at the many church, guru, and power-driven scandals that illustrate this fact, usually with men, the more sexually aggressive gender thanks to testosterone. But in confined quarters, females get plenty tough about *their bitches*, I quickly discovered.

One day in yoga class I tell the girls about the arousal of the spiritual energy, the Kundalini, and how the poses of yoga help us explore, activate, and nurture that divine energy all humans have within them.

"Say wha'?" that day's new girl grimaces as she sits in our circle. "Wha' the heck is she sayin'?" making all of us laugh our heads off. Then I explain to Victoria the difference between the sexual, which she certainly knows about, and the spiritual energy she claims she's never heard of. And its name, Kundalini, well, we all know what she mistook that word for. Easy to get them confused, these similar-sounding words, the name of spiritual energy and the sexual act so familiar to females in lockup.

Sex or spirit, let's face it—religion, conquest, partying, even sports or working out—these forces can overtake us as any other type of addiction can. Acting badly, being depressed, exercising, self-inflicting harm or dangerous behavior can all be addictive. Especially to teens who don't yet know how to love or to control their passions. Acting well or badly is a choice we all make. To the girls in lockup, their crimes were the result of their addictions, behavior patterns that began in childhood. The only way to stop an addiction is to first become aware of it, not be in denial about it. And then—to replace a bad addiction with a good one.

My role at the academy was to share the uplifting practices I'd learned so the girls could have alternatives, better choices. I demonstrated powerful lessons for them, such as how to maintain a connection to the sacred throughout ordinary daily life. This is why I wanted to teach yoga and meditation to these girls. If Kara my stepdaughter, wasn't interested, I could at least try to help these girls, who reminded me so much of my former bad girl self.

Anyone with a harmful habit needs to have a crash, a bottom, in order to be shaken from the false reality that what they're caught up in is *good for them*. In Twelve Step programs this is called a bottom, yet sometimes there may be many, before hard-headed addicts, such as myself, decide to change. I had more than my share of bad experiences before I hit the bottom I needed.

For me I needed a spiritual low, not just a physical one (oh, I had many of those!) and a few mental ones (yes, I lost my marbles, are they back yet?). I never went into details about my story with the yoga girls. But I answered specific questions when they asked. It was good for them to know that someone who'd struggled as much as they did, could survive and even flourish.

One day, I'd given my spiritual awakening spiel, explaining "that's why we do yoga, besides having a good workout. And if we continue a yoga practice," I said, "we get happier. It's just what happens when we work with the power of yoga. We begin to see the *power within* our own selves. We truly realize that heaven or hell can exist within our own Being, right here and now."

Suddenly a new girl named Marybeth shot back to me, "Yeah, well, I don't believe you!"

Usually a girl who signs up to come, wants to be there. But everything that could possibly happen, happens sooner or later when you're teaching at-risk teenage girls. Marybeth turned out to be a major anomaly in our class.

"That's not what the Bible says," she defiantly proclaimed. "It's a sin to say heaven or God is inside me."

Two others—one I knew was highly religious, and the other, a bit cynical—mumbled their agreement with Marybeth. Plainly suspicious, filled with the righteousness of fundamentalism, or maybe from a lifelong unbelief in anything not fed them by parents, church, or State, Marybeth turned to Denise and Kim and said, "Miss T talks shit!"

I was wondering when this clash between Eastern-Western ideologies would come.

And here it was. The Voice of Dissent among the group of us honoring the sacred within as best we could. Under the stringent constraints of a sterile institution filled with anxious and resentful girls, who wanted nothing more than to bust out of there and get high, get laid, and get back to their party temporarily interrupted by the State of Florida—the room froze at this confrontation.

"Marybeth," I said, "I'm going to ask you to just try trusting me about this power within, okay? It's your first class, and I know it may sound weird, but if you keep coming back, you'll understand what I mean. And you'll actually feel that power start to operate in your life. Calming you, making the intolerable, more tolerable. So for now, let's continue. We discuss concerns at every opening circle, so next time please come and ask any questions you have then. But it's time for our poses, and we don't want to miss any part of the physical workout the other girls really enjoy."

Marybeth nodded, begrudgingly. For now, she'd be quiet. For the record, I lost her. She never returned to class. But this suspicion and mistrust would reappear in other girls, until soon Ursula and I decided we had to do what we called "damage control." After certain religious volunteer ladies started appearing at ABG, some of the stricter religious girls showed such agitation, Ursula told me they exhibited signs of deep-seated fear, a trauma that results from extremist doctrine of all kind. "This is more like brain-washing in my professional opinion," Ursula said shaking her head. We would see these girls' fear of not going to heaven reach overdrive each time the visiting evangelical women arrived. The girls related how those well-meaning women claimed, "Yoga and anything Eastern like meditation is evil, of the dark arts. It's the occult." Marybeth's comment was only the first harbinger of the hard work Ursula and I had laid out for us.

Marybeth had harsh words for me when she left that day. She turned her back to me and Mr. Lawrence as she left for her next class, announcing in a loud voice: "I'm not risking my soul for your dumb class. Good-bye and good riddance! I get all the self-empowerment I need from reading the Bible. Everything else will get me thrown into hell, just like my Preacher back home said!"

The most important part of our class was the deep meditation period at the end. Everything else led up to this quiet time, when the girls got to experience their true nature, at their center. When relaxed and guided-to-within, the girls realized, on their own, that everything I told them made sense.

"Meditation is the icing on top of our yummy yoga cake," one girl wrote in our journal.

When they let go of thinking, the girls' spirits had a chance to assimilate what their stressed-out bodies and minds couldn't yet decipher—that we all can choose how we feel, every minute of our day.

During meditation, each person has their own unique inner experience, I told them. "The essence of it is to not talk back to a thought that appears in your stilled mind. And that takes practice. Pretend a thought is a butterfly flitting across your blue-sky mind. Just watch it till it disappears. That's all. There's no need to talk to the butterfly."

Sometimes we briefly shared our experiences afterwards. No two meditations are ever alike.

Each girl who returned to yoga had, at one time or another, entered class feeling low, mad, sad, or anxious. Yet after completing a few rounds of deep breathing, then some poses, they melted into the delicious, ease-full state of meditation. There, the reward was a deep inner release from the worst of life's troubles. For a while, at least, life's problems didn't exist, only inner peace. Every student left with a smile on her face, as if she had nothing to fear. Refreshed.

"Open heart, open mind," as one girl wrote in Yoga Thoughts. "I want to stay like this forever."

CHAPTER 15

the inevitable awaits

Friday the 13th

Charley's eye destroyed Port Charlotte, then headed for Fort Ogden, fifteen miles farther north. Like a magnet attracted to its mother lode, the storm's path was now following the natural earth-indentation of the Peace River corridor, which extends for hundreds of miles straight up central Florida from the river delta that begins in the middle of Port Charlotte Harbor. Back home in St. Pete, relieved to be with her husband and son, Ursula watches Charley's projected path on TV and panics. She reaches for her flip-top, radio-to-radio cell phone and makes her 12,000[th] call to ABG.

"How're the girls doing, Estelle?"

"Same as they done fifteen minutes ago when you called last time, Miss Ursula. Mr. Eric helping keep everyone together. We hear on the TV how Charley-eye smashing up everywhere. I be letting the girls sit right in front of the set so she can see that big fat eye of Charley for her own self. We just hope and pray it ain't coming right toward us. Lord Almighty! These thick walls are startin' to shake in their boots, Miss Ursula, just thinkin' 'bout that!"

Each time a new girl wandered into our yoga class I'd ask if she had any life aspirations. "To be a momma," was the most common reply. Surely it was the most familiar job description they knew, with motherhood considered a truly worthy career choice, the only role most girls in prison can imagine doing when grown up, in this demographic of lack and disenfranchisement.

"Well, there are other possibilities," I always offer. "I'm here to show you how to empower yourselves. But change happens only if you want it. As a recovering person myself, I'm here to show you how to lift yourself up. It all starts here," I point to my heart.

At first a new girl would stare in disbelief when I said this. But, as time went on and they saw me showing up week after week, month after month, year after year, offering simple solutions for their complicated feelings, their dark moods and even darker fears—the slurred muttering, "*She's crazy!*" was steadily replaced by silent trust.

Ursula told me, "It's because you show up each week. Your yoga girls, and the rest in the community who watch you come and go, lugging that big bag of facecloths and carrying that old boom box, they see you truly believe in empowerment. Just by regularly coming to practice yoga with them, you demonstrate how powerful yoga is. Believe me, they notice that you're always in a good mood, and the exercises have made your body strong. It all adds up in their impressionable minds."

Eventually, the girls, even non-yoga girls, warmed up to me. By my coming back each week, everyone grew to trust the strange, copper-haired lady who taught them weird but wonderfully wacky things.

"It's all right here," I again point to my heart, "inside each of us. Let's connect to that center with our breath, shall we?" Each week I'd invite them: "Let's feel that inner place vibrate inside as we make the sound of *Om*. We'll be actors and *pretend* to feel the gears of our awareness shift, deep within us."

I bring my hands together at my heart. And the girls do, too.

Charley, a dervish monster insanely twirling on itself, is sending out from its eye tornadoes and sustaining winds of over 145 mph, ravaging everything in its path. A little more than two hours ago it slammed into Punta Gorda and Port Charlotte, two cities separated by only seven miles, before heading up the Peace River basin. Houses on both sides of the river fly apart like matchsticks. Roofs spin like discuses thrown by cosmic giants. People shiver and shake and burrow deeper in their hiding places. Madness has been unleashed on the Gulf of Mexico side of Florida.

Charley's path, if it continues on this inland course, will veer across the entire state at a southwest-to-northeast angle. Everyone along the projected course begins to realize this is Charley's sad song for central Florida. People scurrying to prepare for the inevitable know anything is possible.

One day Porscha, a fifteen-year-old with a complicated hair design of fine African-inspired braids cascading in all directions, asked more about "getting this control stuff" when given the card on which I'd hand-written, *Letting-go*. Sitting in our circle the girls and I were discussing this recurring topic that always interested them. On this particular day, Jane has picked the card *Self-esteem* and she wants to know "how to get it." I tell the new girls, Porscha and Jane, the two topics are interrelated and our discussion proceeds to focus on them. No one objected. They agreed that the other cards drawn—*Curiosity, Willingness, Trust*—would have to wait for another day's rap session.

"When I first noticed this," I said, talking of this concept that came up nearly every week, "it seemed as if the only people who don't get into controlling others, or don't allow themselves to be controlled by others, are those whose lives have become spiritualized. That's the word I prefer, *spiritualized*, instead of *awakened*."

"I'm confused," Porscha moaned.

"Okay, here's how it happened for me. One day—after bottoming out—I was sick and tired of life. I just couldn't take the emotional pain anymore. So I chose to put down my drug and alcohol addictions by joining the spiritual fellowship of AA. Coincidently—exactly then!—I met the perfect spiritual teacher for me. And I've stayed with her now for the last twenty-two years. Through both the getting-sober program of AA and my spiritual teacher's ancient yogic wisdom, I was able to change my life. I learned about boundaries, which included the lesson to not allow others to control me. Deciding to stop abusing myself and to start cultivating a spiritual life was the beginning of gaining control of my own Self. I *had* to put down my negative addictions in order to start building up my self-esteem. Mine was less than zero, you see. I was a weekend teenage drunk by fifteen; sound familiar, you guys? Drugs weren't that available when I was growing up, it was practically in the Dark Ages."

Lakendra loudly reacted to this, collapsing her body into a dramatic heap of confusion. She hadn't the foggiest idea of what was going on. "I don't know one word 'bout what you saying, but it relaxes me, Miss. It takes away my stress," Lakendra said, expressing the sentiment shared by many girls who kept coming back to class. But whether it was only that one time to see it wasn't for them, or deciding to come back regularly, everyone felt less troubled by the end of our session. Jane's question on how to boost her self-worth received the most attention that day.

"How do I know what's best for my self-esteem, Miss?" she asked.

"That's a great question, Jane. And one only you can answer. The best indicator is how your gut feels. You know, how comfortable in your own skin you feel when deciding you will, or you won't do something," I replied. "Our *gut* is the way our conscience *speaks* to us. You know when you're doing something right or not, am I correct?"

Jane nodded her head, as did everyone there.

"And when you feel good inside, with no fear, no guilt—that's a strong sign you're on the right track. Every time you feel good, you've made another *right* choice. That's how you boost your self-image. That's how you feel better and better about yourself."

"Okay, I get it," Jane said. "Like how, when I snorted some crank I felt shitty before I even did it," she said and looked around at the others. Everyone mumbled their agreement. Only in yoga class and in the House Meetings Ursula supervised can the girls talk so openly about their old using-days. "When I quit, after I got busted, I felt sick, yeah, but y'know I felt good I wasn't using no more."

"That's a perfect example of how to take control of yourself, and build up your self-esteem, Jane. Very good."

Jane asked a few more questions and other girls offered their opinions. This is how it goes, no teaching, just sharing personal truths. Our group discussions were always of-the-moment. They were usually based on whatever situation a girl faced right then at the academy. Or a card any of the girls drew to start the conversation. The cards inspired talks on:

Surrender/Openness
Sisterhood/Brotherhood
Patience
Abundance
Forgiveness
Synethesis
Love
Joy
Hope

At every session, a basic spiritual attribute was discussed as casually as other teens might discuss what movie they saw, what tune was on the radio, what cute guy or gal called. How these subjects related to each girl's life—that's what we talked about.

"I ain't got no patience!"

"I could use a little lovin' right now," drew many, "Yeah me, too," responses.

"Syntha-what?"

"Synethesis," I'd say. "Everything coming together, naturally."

Everyone became a little more self-aware with each week's discussion. Things that were never noticed before—got noticed now.

"I'm feeling less stressed!"

"I want to understand how the girls I'm pissed at feel, so I can get along better with them and stop fighting so much."

"Yeah, I used to have lots of criticals, but—I stopped getting them since I've been thinking about why I need so much attention."

In just a few minutes of sharing about positive qualities gleaned from the illustrated slips of cardboard, we would have an instant, full-blown yogic-philosophy discourse, sometimes dramatized instead of the girls' usual acting-out. This was our peer-designed self-help therapy. My role was merely that of a facilitator. I never told anyone what to do in our circles. Together, we'd figure it out. And then it was time to do the poses.

Looking back, I now see that these discussions were more dialogue than anything. The cards posed the question. The girls related the topic to their lives, their particular situation. I listened closely, adding only a suggestion here or there.

"All the wisdom any of us ever needs is within," I reminded them whether the exchange got heated, confused, at loose ends, or dove smoothly into profound waters. "Knowing how to access our so-groovy, so-present inner wisdom—and remembering we have it—that's the tricky part."

The girls who returned each week saw their lives change in this stress-filled place. Dry and needy sponges, each of my yoga gals soaked up the topics we discussed, like how to:

Practice discrimination (Learning to say the hardest word in the English language, "No.")

Let go and let good (Dropping the need to always be in control, or controlled by another.)

Fake it till you make it (My favorite, often followed by, "the best way to be happy—just pretend! And smile! Pretty soon ... you aren't mad or sad or scared anymore.")

The girls learned how to breathe, contemplate, repeat simple phrases, make affirmations, calm their minds, and perform challenging yoga poses. But most importantly—ending each and every class—they enjoyed their meditative deep relaxation time.

Katy, or Kali as she was called in class, hadn't missed a session since she returned from her binge, quickly accepting her substantial extra time added on for running away. A spark of interest was now permanently etched on her face by the third class since returning. Her druggy hangover gone, her fury over getting caught, dissolved. Now she wanted to prove she was a good person, and ready to be a good mom, too. A new, gentle look of peace replaced her former arrogant smirk that once smeared her good looks. Even though she'd been a regular since I first started teaching at the academy, a year before she absconded, she always had a "holier than thou" attitude. Now truly a devoted student, Kali was transformed. She became vocal about being in the *yoga groove*.

"Since you mentioned the possibility of being a yoga teacher, Miss, I suddenly feel good about myself, like I might have a future," she said in our circle one day.

I wanted to explore Kali's experience with the others, with Kali's permission, of course. "When someone realizes there's more going on than what appears to be true—that's the kind of groove you want to be in. It all starts with willingness to be humble. Not humiliated, but humble. To really *know* something, we have to tell ourselves we *don't know anything.* The wise-guy yoga sages say: *Those who know, don't know. Those who don't know, know.*"

"Say wha'?! You don't be making no sense, Miss!" I looked over to Brittany, our new girl that day, who couldn't get out of her giggly, eye-rolling *this is too weird for me* headset. Sadly, she was another girl who only attended one time.

"What have you got to lose?" I said, trying to coax Laronda, the next new girl who showed up. She acted as if she'd been ordered to come to class but I knew that anyone who signed up did so voluntarily. I had to remind her that she was dead wrong after she rudely greeted me saying, "You're just some white lady who feels sorry for us."

"I don't have to be here, you know, Laronda. I have art to make, books to write, a business to run, plus a family to raise. I'm here because I want to give you guys what I didn't get at your age. No one showed me how to tap into this power within my own Being. Nobody, until I ran into a teacher when I was in my thirties. Don't tell me you're forced to come here. You signed up, just like all the other girls here. So hush up, open your ears, let the others have their special time, they deserve it—or you can leave now. You're welcome to go. No skin off my nose."

The rest of the girls stared hard at Laronda, aggravated that this girl, full of doubt, uncouth, and boldface lying that she had no choice in coming to class, was causing a delay to their precious yoga time. I knew there were always going to be disrupters in our constantly rotating attendees. But to the regulars—Laronda's behavior was outrageous. I noticed their annoyance. I also knew how peer pressure works. There was no need for me to say anything more to Laronda. I figured she would get a mouthful later on. It had happened before.

I turned my attention to the regulars. "You guys don't have many opportunities to move those soft bodies of yours, that's why you're so stiff. Come on, take off those socks!" The regulars immediately shifted their emotional gears from anger at Laronda, to giggling at my outlandishness, nodding their heads, and pointing at a few pairs of sock-clad feet. Two girls removed their socks while Laronda refused to take hers off. She grimaced and snorted.

"Believe me," I said, ignoring Laronda, "keep coming back to yoga and you'll see some real changes. First your body starts to feel firmer, tingling with energy in places you never knew you had before. Those are called muscles, girls. Everyone wants their blubber to turn into muscle. Right, Porscha?"

Porscha shouted, "I lost ten pounds already! My self-esteem is high as the sky now!"

"When your abs start to get tight," I continued, "then your weak backs don't ache anymore. And if you keep coming back, your mind becomes more focused, calmer just by learning how to do these poses. Give yourself credit that you're achieving a difficult challenge. Before you know it, you'll experience real happiness, for no other reason than that you're alive. Self-discipline is the best way to build self-respect. Right, Porscha? That's what happens when you do these exercises regularly."

"Yeah, right," Laronda murmured sarcastically.

"Shhhh," the others told her. "Just try it, Laronda! She's not kidding."

When we sounded the three *Oms* signaling it was time to *change focus*, Laronda's expected giggle-chord accompanied the other combined voices that were harmonious and sincere. For my five regulars in attendance, the difference was palpable.

"When I do my first *Om*," Alex/Durga wrote in the class journal, "it feels like I'm ending the rotten time of feeling bad. That sound Om we make tells me I'm ready to start feeling better. That good feeling is now real to me. I never knew it before coming here, doing yoga with you. The change inside my body always comes at our very first Om. I look forward to it, and sure enough, peace happens! Every time we start, I feel happier from the first deep breath I take to make my Om sound."

Om ... gently cradles our hearts

CHAPTER 16

practice, practice, practice

By the time I returned to the academy after, what was to me, an insignificant incident with Laronda, Ursula greeted me with some interesting news.

"Wish you could have been at our House Meeting the day after last week's classes, teZa," she said with a big grin on her face. "You'd be amazed by what happened. The regular girls from your class, Alex, Katy, Shay, Tiffany, Gail, and some of the others brought up how disruptive Laronda was, and how she almost ruined the entire class for everybody with her bad attitude."

"Really? Wow, I'm surprised," I said. "Laronda's behavior didn't seem that unusual to me. Lots of new girls come to class wearing fears and prejudices right on their sleeves."

"Well, this time your regulars called Laronda out on it," Ursula beamed. "They started off that day's meeting, right away, by saying they're sick of new girls showing up just to scoff at them. They want the entire population at ABG to know it's not fair. They said they're desperate to change, and your class is their biggest pleasure all week long. And guess what?"

"I can't imagine."

"Laronda ended up apologizing not only to the yoga girls, but to the entire school, for not having an open mind when she signed up for yoga class."

"She did? I'm surprised. She didn't seem the type to ever admit her shortcomings."

"Well, the other girls shamed her into it, I guess. There was a lot of hot words in a back-and-forth. Laronda tried to defend her attitude, but in the end, the girls put pressure on her. The yoga girls did invite her back, if she wanted to return. They said what they've got going with you, learning about Self-empowerment, can't be jeopardized by what they called *spies*. I think that's funny, that they thought Laronda was a plant, meant to purposely disrupt their yoga time."

"Well, it might be true," I said. "She sure acted like she didn't want to be there. But I admire any girl who's brave enough to step into something so new and different as our class. Especially these girls who don't know anything about serenity, or a quiet life, Eastern or any other way, any form of higher understanding besides rap and hip-hop. I'm surprised more spies aren't showing up, from what happened with the fundamentals, the hardcore religious girls who always challenge us."

Ursula said, "I gave Laronda a flower to represent letting-go and suggested she put it up on the altar, from a bouquet I'd been given by one of my co-workers. Then I gave each of the yoga girls a flower, too. Put this on our community altar, I told them, and let it symbolize your acceptance of Laronda's apology for diss-ing you guys who try so hard to better yourselves in yoga. Each time you see the altar with your acceptance-flowers on it, all of you will remember how big your heart is, that you can ask for, and receive, forgiveness."

Ursula's handling of this potentially humiliating situation for Laronda impressed me. She turned the girls' confrontation at the House Meeting around by using plain chrysanthemums as symbols of intention, both of self-acknowledgement (Laronda's letting-go) and forgiveness (by the others). The flowers, together in a water-bottle vase, had become teaching tools. Each time any of the girls saw them on the altar, they remembered that differences can be resolved with love instead of hatred. The girls' simple altar signified their hearts radiating love and nonviolent resolution. It gave the girls hope. The colorful, fragrant flowers symbolized the win-win attitude of peaceful understanding instead of what was the standard before: selfishly flung barbs of hurt and mean-spirited trouble, ruining things for everybody.

Best of all was Laronda's coming back to class that very next week. She arrived and immediately picked the yoga name Leela, the *playfulness of God*. Her attitude had done a one-eighty-degree turn. Instead of scoffing and eye-rolling, Leela listened to all the instructions: for deep breathing, Om-ing, doing poses, and going into our final meditation. She went so deep into the silence of her inner power that by the end of our Thursday session, the former skeptic loudly exclaimed, "I'm happier than when I got here!" and left smiling, as opposed to wearing the pickle-puss face she'd arrived with the week before.

Other girls tried bullying their way into class. But now the regulars were the ones who quickly put a stop to this, after Laronda/Leela.

Kali/Katy said it aloud at that opening circle, right after Leela asked for her name. "Never again will girls say they don't believe in the inner power that we yoga girls know is for real, that's why we keep practicing. We're not taking no more showdowns!"

Gail/Dharma chimed in: "That's right! We put it to all us ABG girls to vote, and we won! No scoffing of yoga is ever allowed in class, or anywhere! Miss Ursula said that anyone who makes fun of us loses their privilege to ever participate in class. That's what we voted on."

Tiffany/Omkara added, "We have to make space for the girls who really want to learn about yoga, that's what we told them. And everyone agreed."

There was a lull in our opening circle's excited talk. That's when Alex/Durga added in a very soft voice, "That's why Miss Ursula gave us the flowers to put on the altar."

Only a few weeks later, it would happen again. Cindy, a new girl just arrived for her long sentence, didn't know what was up yet. She signed up for yoga class and right away started laughing at what we do. The other girls told her, "Shut up! We don't put up with no dissin'!"

Cindy, who only wanted to fit in, was shocked at finding her irreverence wasn't considered cool. She'd gone against *the unspoken code* in our opening circle, laughed in all the wrong places, guffawed just too many times, so queen-bee Kali told her to be quiet. Kali was now the alpha-girl in the entire facility. Right away Cindy pleaded loudly, "I'm sorry! Geez, I didn't know yoga was such a big deal to y'all! Please give me a second chance!"

Kali said, "You have a choice, Cindy, either fake it till you make it, stay positive and just listen, or leave now and don't sign up ever again."

"I'll be better, believe me!" Cindy promised.

Shay added, "We must be polite to Miss T for coming here to teach us yoga."

I interrupted the regulars who were running the circle. "I'm just the facilitator here, Cindy. I'm just opening the door so you can walk in on your own. You girls are doing all the work here. I love it!"

"Love what, Miss?" Melanie asked.

"Seeing you dive into your inner selves, enjoying the greatest love affair of your lives," I said. "Learning what it means when we yogis say, 'Gee, You Are You' for guru, our teacher within. Because the best teacher you'll ever find is your own God-given wisdom. You just have to get still enough, quiet enough to hear what your guru, the inner teacher, is trying to tell you."

Before she left that day, Cindy asked for and chose her new yoga name, Grace. "I'm not ready for one of those sandy-skrit ones," she said with a smile. "I like English."

CHAPTER 17

in the *'I'* of me, myself

From Charlotte Harbor, Charley barreled right up the Peace River corridor like an arrow pointing to its invisible mark. The tiny eye of the massive storm system devastated everyone and everything in its path. Hitting like an explosion, flattening anything solid, skipping, skirting, randomly hopping over, plundering, slicing through hard walls, wiping out dirt roads and blowing trails away, flooding highways, erasing landscapes in one sweep—as a hand demolishes a spider's intricate web—it felled, crushed and destroyed roofs, homes, cars, factories, downtowns, uptowns, every which way it could. Charley's surge of whipped water, wind and screeching madness rushed into every nook, every crevice, its ferocity laughing wildly at us puny humans as we watched helplessly.

Such diabolical cacophony—worse than an imagined herd of tyrannosauruses or a full-speed collision of onrushing trains colliding endlessly—could be heard a couple hundred miles up the Peace River corridor. In tiny Bowling Green, its terrified citizens listened to constant weather updates. The battle between Nature and all of God's creatures was in full force. Charley's wreckage began when it hit the continent at the barrier islands, then Punta Gorda and Port Charlotte, and now its aim was directly for—minuscule ABG.

The tiny hamlet of Nocatee is next. The town's citizens have mostly evacuated. Hardly anyone is foolish enough to stay behind. People who couldn't be convinced to leave are huddled in their closet, in their bathroom tub, or the safest interior room, the one with the strongest overhead rafters. The last evacuation notice was enforced hours before the eye's deafening strike.

Charley is now in its nerve-grinding, steady march north, destroying all it can—following the Peace River's antediluvian geological trail that cuts deeply through the belly of Florida.

The eye is heading directly for the minutest speck on any rural map, Bowling Green, where right now Estelle is quietly speaking on her cell to Ursula for the umpteenth time. "I'm telling 'em like you said, Miss Ursula: Y'all must remain calm in the face of that nasty eyeball of Charley the radio and TV people says is comin' right at us, girls."

Traveling 22 mph up the Peace River corridor, Charley may or may not, at any moment, bounce or bop a few degrees to a new course heading. Still—it doesn't look good for Bowling Green.

Ursula speaks to head of security's concerns. "I've seen all the bad stuff on the news, Estelle, but don't worry. I know that structure as well as Rafi's and my own house. You and the girls will be perfectly safe there. You have my word. Rafi came out to inspect the roof just last month, when hurricane season began."

Estelle swallows hard. She trusts her boss. She knows Ursula would never lie to her. Right then she looks outside the bulletproof windows and sees loose branches of the oak across the street fly by. She peers down the street to the trees' strong limbs waving in the wind like fans at a football game. Other loose debris flies in the air, making swirling patterns of leaves, trash, an occasional piece of roofing, shiny-sheared metal. She wonders if it's the really dangerous kind. She remembers hearing stories about people's heads being cut off by rusty old pieces of galvanized sheeting from abandoned barns, slicing through the air like a hailstorm of knife thrower blades at a circus.

Estelle can suddenly smell her own sweat. She takes a dry gulp and her throat feels scratchy. She looks out the window and grips her cell phone as if it's a lifeline.

Outside the window, with Charley's eye inching toward them, the gusts are churning, picking up speed. Every wild animal has already sought shelter wherever it can. Every domesticated one has hopefully been corralled and protected by its owner. Leafy plants have been torn apart; woody trunks are being shredded from their anchored roots. Everything in Bowling Green—in the tornado-strength pre-storm gusts shooting off from far-away Charley's eye—is starting to be blown to smithereens.

The few people who stayed in Fort Ogden are experiencing the final stage of the eye. The front end of the storm hit an hour ago; then the fifteen-minute eerie calm of Charley's eye passed over; then the back end of the storm, with its schizophrenic winds coming from the reverse direction, hit just as hard as the front wall had, with crazy spinoff tornadoes crisscrossing back and forth in this tight zone of a hurricane's core.

The few souls who survived Charley when it rammed into Fort Ogden are just about done-in. The system's double lashing, front and back walls, with Charley's spinning eye in between, is over too soon for the accumulated lifetime of things lots of folks lost. The front end, a full-blown bomb-like extravaganza, lasted almost an hour and did the evil deed of tearing out the heart of people's existence. That front wall wasted in mere minutes generations of human effort—heirlooms, memories, homes, businesses—remnants of which are now part of the swirling debris sucked into and feeding the storm's unstoppable core of energy.

At Nocatee, seven miles from Fort Ogden, those who stayed are now in the middle of the front wall's lashing, a licking that will last another hour before the final burst of Charley's rear wall arrives, after the eye's meager period of blessed stillness.

Fort Ogden and Nocatee are flattened except for the strongest cement-block structures, where inhabitants cowered, figuring rightly they'll be safe. Nobody is foolish enough to attempt riding out the eye's hit in anything but a cement building, which the academy is, in 48 miles-distant Bowling Green.

A peculiarity of every spiraling storm is its vast destructive force coming from two opposite directions, with a small central space in between of preternatural calm. The innermost space of a hurricane is the eye, which to a layman includes the ferocious immediate vicinity, its eyewall.

Every northern hemisphere hurricane travels counterclockwise, with the winds of the front wall coming from the southeast. Then arrives the baffling dead calm at every hurricane's core, where there is virtually no wind. Here there's no whisper of the fierce wild that lies beyond a scant measure, a mile perhaps, away from this center of peace—lasting anywhere from five to twenty minutes, depending on the size and forward-traveling speed of each particular storm. The eye's respite is immediately followed (with no noticeable interlude) by a second onslaught of the circular lashing. Now the wind of the back wall appears to change direction, as it comes from the northwest. But it is the surreal trick of a spiraling typhoon's eye. This phenomenon is noticeable when close to the eye of a hurricane. Whatever the front wall doesn't smash or blast apart, the rear wall demolishes in its one-two knockout.

Most big trees uprooted in a Florida hurricane crash-land facing in a northwesterly direction. This is because the front wall immediately takes the weakened ones down. If a tree isn't done in by the front wall but gives up its tenacious hold on life when the back wall hits, it generally lands facing southeasterly. A hurricane's spinning-top slaughter of these great living beings, the Earth's majestic tall trees, is part of Nature's delicate balance of ridding the terrain of the old to make way for the new. A sad sight, old trees tumbling; the natural selection process not always pleasant to witness.

A hurricane's double-punch wallop, its front and back winds of two opposing, maddening directions, with the freakily calm center, is what one expects when up close to a storm's eye. During the brief time the exact eye travels overhead, no noticeable wind exists in the middle of a storm's axis. There's light rainfall and certainly the sky is ominously overcast. If you are there, being within the very center of a hurricane's rapacious eye is indescribably otherworldly. It's dreamlike and feels uncannily safe to be in such dead silence when you're surrounded by an otherwise deadly tempest. Yes, each nightmarish storm has—seemingly contradictory to the nature of killer-storms—an utterly peaceful inner core.

CHAPTER 18

stronger?
storm's eye or our *'I'*

We're again sitting in our opening circle on Thursday before Charley is due to hit our region, sometime tomorrow.

"Girls, your inner *'I'* is where you can go whenever you need comfort. If you're scared, mad, or sad, or just need to feel connected—go within. Follow one conscious breath and you're there. Listen to your own breathing coming in deeply, going out long. Tune out the constant voice that rattles on, the chatter of your mind. That bothersome monkey-mind comes from things outside of you. It's not really who you are.

"The real you is your inner core of immeasurable power. Once you go through the necessary purification stage—in which you face, not run from your fears—that inner place is complete stillness.

"And guess what?" I say in an excited tone. "This peace within each human being is as real as the eye of every hurricane. It's just that most people don't believe their inner *'I'* exists, or haven't come to trust it yet. Some people don't get to know it until someone else introduces them to it."

I take a loud deep breath in, and let the girls watch me slowly exhale.

"Allow me to introduce you to the most powerful friend, and the healthiest relationship you'll ever have—one with your own inner *'I'*."

The girls remain silent and look at each other with wide, eager eyes.

I nod my head. "That's right. Charley's eye, which might or might not hit us tomorrow, just might turn out to be an enjoyable, life-altering experience, if you decide to stay protected inside your safe inner *'I'*. *R*emember, stay in that sacred inner place, and pay no attention to the outside hullaballoo that tries to distract us from who we really are."

right effort: the nectar of life

Months earlier, Heather pulled the card marked *Contentment* from the bag each girl was to choose from randomly, although I noticed them putting back cards until they found one they really liked.

Heather said, "I get into the yoga groove as soon as I sit in our circle. It makes me smile so hard to be here, even if I'm mad when I step in here."

She wanted a second card, and I never say no. Heather pulled out the card *Effort*. I asked her what she thought it meant in her life. "I guess I have to work more, if I want more contentment."

I smiled and said, "You guys are getting the hang of this inner-wisdom stuff. I'm impressed. Isn't it great that you can tap what's inside—whenever you need it!"

Molly had returned that day for her second class. A thin, sad girl who, at seventeen, had a baby at home she constantly fretted about. Molly sat in silence, angrily staring into my eyes. I understood from her comments the week before, when she chose the name Matrika (*the spiritual power of words*), that she suspected I was a phony, that yoga was hokey, and everything I told the girls was just made-up BS. I noticed her searching for any sign that I was a liar. Last week during our sharing circle she said, "I've never been happy. I don't believe happiness exists." The other yoga girls urged Molly to keep coming back to "Miss T's class."

Sarah jauntily jumped in and said, "Each week yoga completely changes my mood. The staff calls it anger management, you know. Look at me! You know how pissed-off and disgusted I can get." The other girls laughed vigorously nodding their heads. They knew all too well the fallout of Sarah's bad moods.

Everyone did a double-take when they heard her next say, "It's a waste of my energy to be mad anymore."

Sarah's shift had been nothing short of wondrous. I loved seeing the girls lap up the benefits of practicing yoga regularly. As I told each new girl: "When we go to our inner wisdom, it's like we're planting seeds for a happy life. It only takes *wanting* to accept more happiness in life. Anyone can choose that. Even if they're behind bars, like you guys."

In just a few sessions, Molly, now Matrika in class, will be another "girl-miracle" as I call my regulars. Before yoga, they were anything but happy; after yoga instructions, they're all smiles, accepting their less-for-now life, *as it is*. Then, setting a goal to get better, one step at a time. Part of the healing process we do is visualizing our happier, higher selves.

As long as they kept coming back, every formerly pissed-off, feeling-unloved girl started to experience real happiness. "For no reason," as Molly/Matrika now exclaimed in an opening circle, "after that one class, I felt—free inside. I don't know how it works, but ... this here yoga shit is my new drug of choice, Miss."

In the corner, Mr. Lawrence glanced up from his hissing walkie-talkie. He was used to the strange language spoken during yoga class. He let me run the show, never handing out any criticals in front of me. Everyone knew how fond he was of dishing them out. Lawrence's laziness was as well-known as was his tendency to be grouchy.

Matrika soon became one of the most zealous of the yoga girls, returning each week, writing in our group diary.

During her eight-month stay Matrika contributed many entries in *Yoga Thoughts*. Here's a selection:

- Yoga helps me see that I can choose to get better, right here and now.
- It's hard, so hard sometimes! But when I get a pose right I feel so good about myself. I know I can do this!
- The best way I can help my baby back home is by getting myself straightened out.
- Yoga is the best thing I've learned while in here.
- I can think clearer, thanks to the poses. I feel less confused after doing all this focusing stuff.
- While I'm doing a pose, my brain shuts off. I'm busy watching my breath, getting my body in the right position. I have peace then. Maybe if I keep this up, I'll get more peace.
- I want to plant those thought-seeds, like Miss T calls them, inside me. Happiness seeds.

Months before Charley we're in class one day. "What we do here is tap our inner wisdom," I said, "where everyone's real power lies. That way you learn to control your inner self. Then nobody and no-*thing* can hurt you. Stay in your inner *'I'* and not even the guards, or the judge who sent you here, can affect your happiness. They may have the keys to your prison doors, but it's only you who determines how happy you are, not anyone else. The truest kind of happy is how you feel inside, not the feeling based on what's happening on the outside."

New girls usually rolled their eyes or shook their heads, and every once in a while a girl's voice boomed in total disbelief:

"Say wha'?!" "What she talkin' 'bout anyway?" "What kind of honkey bullshit you doin' in here?"

We'd laugh and glance over at Mr. Lawrence, who pretended he was busy listening to his walkie-talkie, not hearing our sex-and-drug talk, although it wasn't exactly academy procedure. Twice, when I couldn't handle a troublemaker who acted out, even after the Laronda confrontation, I had to say: "Mr. Lawrence, will you please radio the office that so-and-so has to go back to her other activity." That either stopped the misbehavior cold, or the girl left, returning to her unhappy, self-imposed misery.

Matrika, by her third class, became a self-proclaimed yoga girl. She confided to the next new girl, a tough gang girl like herself, the same advice she got when she first joined our circle of twelve. "It happened to me, feeling free. So it's true for me. That's all I'm saying." Once a disgruntled skeptic, now a convert, Molly delighted in playing teacher's aide with such open honesty.

The longer the same girls kept coming back to class the less I had to say. The regulars all became my assistants. They "got it" and wanted to share it. Happiness is contagious.

"When you plant the seeds of wanting joy," I reminded them as we did our poses, "your radar is automatically set on getting just that. In yoga we call this the 'wish-fulfilling tree.' That means what you sow, you reap. If you are constantly disturbed, you'll never be free. If you learn to accept life for what it is, then you have a shot at true happiness."

"Wait, Miss! How can I accept that my daddy's a drug addict and he beat me?" Shay asked.

"That's all hurtful, for sure, Shay. To accept it means that you protect yourself, even call the cops if you have to. You accept that your daddy's an abuser, but you don't accept the abuse. Learning to discriminate, to tell the difference, is what happens when we tap this inner wisdom I'm always telling you about, the knowledge that comes the more you do yoga."

"Uh, okay. I get that. So I just run, right? And accept I have to run, and not accept getting a busted lip."

"That's about it. Maybe run to a friend's house or a relative's, or call 911 if you're really scared, and ask for help. That's being smart, accepting that you have a challenging situation at home. One that's clearly, absolutely unacceptable. Your way of accepting life as it is, is to run from or try to end the abuse. Get away, go as far and as fast as you can. But ... you have to accept that your father's like this. That's how we forgive both ourselves and our abusers. We distance ourselves, go to a place of safety, and then we can reconcile ourselves to people's bad behavior when we acknowledge who they really are. We don't expect them to be different. But we protect ourselves from their harming us. That way, you accept your dad's inadequacies, and you also accept that you have power to change the situation. You can get out of his way!"

Other girls asked more questions about this subject. It was fascinating to them that they could take full control of their lives, by only desiring it.

"Yes, being in control of your own inner life, how you feel—is your birthright. It's a seed that grows within you, from the moment you take your first breath. Every human has the potential to tap this power. By consciously breathing, doing yoga poses, focusing on positives, and practicing stilling the mind with meditation—all these nourish the seeds of happiness within us."

I looked around our circle. Every girl's face had a pleased, expectant smile. It made me feel good to know that I was sharing this inner wealth, a veritable heavenly kingdom, with these girls who so desperately needed all the love they could get. They'd been given tough hands to play in the game of life. I felt for them. I related to them. And I knew that, like me, all they had to do was decide to change and their spirits would lift. I took a deep breath and continued.

"The best way for anyone to trust this concept of being free and being happy," I add, "is to see for yourselves. So here we go! Let's start with *pranayama*, our breathing exercise. Then we'll stand and begin with the mountain pose, and then our five warm-up sun salutes. Okay, ready?"

CHAPTER 20

stormy or sunny—our choice

"*Namaste*," I say to the girls and they cheerily repeat it right back to me.

"Namaste," everyone says in unison, facing Mr. Lawrence, in our ritual greeting of one another, including any staff on duty during that class.

"Have a *nice day*," he hisses back repeatedly. We're all used to his curmudgeon-y ways. It doesn't faze us at all. We laugh at Lawrence's sarcastic response. We don't care. We expect nothing more from this sour-faced dude. Now all of us turn to our immediate neighbor, as I've taught them. The girls bow and "Namaste" to those on either side.

Three new students are in class today, giggling nervously, as girls always do when they first arrive. We're sitting in our tight circle on the floor. Matrika has taken it upon herself to fetch our inspiration-cards out of my tote bag and has passed them around, having drawn out two for herself. She always likes to take two. I used to think it was because she was afraid the first wouldn't be good enough, but eventually I caught on: her thinking is that the second gives her deeper insight into the meaning of the first. I smile at knowing this young woman looks to my handmade cards for a *hint* or a *door into* the place that's becoming more accessible to her—insight into her own inner Self. All new girls who arrive at yoga class lack this trait. But a girl who keeps coming back receives an abundance of *aha*-moments, or heightened perceptions, as fast as she can open up her eager young mind.

"This seat of curiosity," I say, "is your inner *'I'*. Maybe the *'I'* really stands for *Insight*, not just the normal me-myself-and-I."

Also present today is Kali, always eager to practice yoga. She's one of seven regulars who've signed up, even with a conflict in today's regularly scheduled classes. The competition isn't the fundamental Christians, or the AA or NA volunteers who hold weekly meetings, but a Girl Scouts representative, who showed up on a wrong date with an art project. Rather than turn her away, Ursula let the woman hold her special workshop, knowing my class would have less-than-normal attendance. Ursula tells me later, "Less is sometimes more, when it comes to spiritual practice. Let's face it, teZ, most teenage girls would rather make tchotchkes, some wood plaque with their name spelled out in varicolored beans and seeds, than do the physical effort of getting into poses, and then meditating."

I give Kali, Matrika, Shay, Eternia, Durga, Maya, Marybeth, and three new girls a Xeroxed paper of stick-figure drawings of the poses we'll be doing today. *Warrior I & II, the Dancer, Crescent Moon, Rabbit, Side Twist* and … *yogic abs,* every girl's nemesis. Any young woman who has the intention of ever wearing a two-piece to the beach again on the Outs, grows to appreciate the ab workouts we do, coordinated with breath, of course, as we focus on abdominals.

Along with words of encouragement about how yoga not only builds strong bodies, steady minds and a shiny spirit, I include on the sheet a saying I often quote in class, with a nod and a chuckle:

Yoginis wear bikinis!

For every girl at the academy, life itself has become one big bad storm. That's why they received their sentence from the court.

I look at the ten girls in today's circle. "You didn't end up here because your attitudes were great." They all laugh in agreement.

I continue, "As I've mentioned before, when someone's chosen to wake up from living half-asleep, and elevated their spirit—it can be a double-edged sword. That means we have to work for what we want. If we want peace, we have to let go of our need to control. This is what the ancient yoga saying means: *Being awake and aware* (conscious) *is like walking along a razor's edge.*"

I look around and see eyebrows lift with interest. The girls love dangerous talk. This aphorism is graphic and extreme, and true. Naturally, they want to hear more.

"This often-used quote," I say, "comes from a thousands-year-old verse, called a *sutra*, of the *Rig Veda*, a yogic scripture. The point is vivid, isn't it," I ask and they loudly agree. "To become *awake*—to sharpen our senses, our awareness of what life's really about—takes being vigilant. Often life situations demand our attention to be vigilant. The more we look, the more we see or perceive. Awareness is like walking along a razor's edge, the ancient sages explained, in this strange phrase that appeared in the earliest holy books of Eastern origin."

"Ain't that dangerous, Miss, walking on a razor?" Shay asks.

"Yeah, it sounds like if you slip you might get sliced in two," Matrika says.

"What does it mean, Miss? 'to walk the razor's edge'?" Valerie, one of the new girls, asks. "That sounds awful dangerous."

"It means much more than danger," I said, smiling. "For some, it's impossible. Lots of people can't find the balance of having a spiritual and an ordinary life. When things are on 'the edge' or 'edgy' that usually means something that not everyone commonly can, or wants to do. It's not exactly as popular to be a spiritual person, is it, as it is to be a rap artist or football star?

"Spiritual people are often unconventional. It takes a certain amount of courage to take the road less traveled, as living from heightened perceptions is sometimes described. To not play the control-or-be-controlled game that most people do, without knowing they're doing it—that's the ordinary way of life. But to believe that this world, right here, is a spiritual journey we're all on together—not just a make-babies, work-and-die struggle—*that's edgy*.

"Having a spiritual life is believing that things are not what they appear to be. Walking on the edge of a razor takes way more courage than just accepting what we can see, hear, and touch right in front of us. Always remember, girls: our own life is a reality show that we get to make into whatever we want of it."

"Say what?" Shay interrupts as she tends to do, being bolder than the other regulars. "Life is too hard to be anything most times but a drag! C'mon, Miss! This yoga's making my abs like steel, but spiritual? That I ain't." The other girls loudly erupt into conflicted shouts at ShakespearesDelight's confession.

When they quiet down Kali, the fiercest of yoga girls, says, "Some of us want more in our lives than just eating, making babies, and going to work. So, tell us, Miss."

The girls look at one another with murmurs of *yeah, right on.* I'm glad I've been invited to speak in depth about such a profound subject. I consider Shay, one of my favorites, to be the jester of our group, always laughing and challenging everything we discuss.

"The path to happiness," I begin, "is lined with challenges and hazards. Only the strong of heart have the courage to follow it. To seek the spiritual, I mean. The rest of us simply get by, perhaps only making a change in the physical: one's hair, weight, love interest, buying a new outfit or set of wheels. It takes determination and effort to change longtime habits, where our attitudes originate from. Instead of being courageous to change, many people deny, or aggressively cling to their negative attitudes, out of psychic laziness. We decide to change only when discomfort outweighs the burden of our old familiar comfort zone. And I would say you guys here, at ABG, are definitely eligible for that category."

"What you mean, Miss?" Vonda, a new girl, asks, her befuddlement obvious on her face.

"I mean that you guys are being given an opportunity to change."

"How's that?"

"Because you got caught. You're here. You're not on the streets still using or stealing. You're forced to face your destiny. You're being given an opportunity to slow down and see that your beliefs and ways of thinking can be redirected so you can have a better life. But only if you choose to do so."

The circle bursts into a buzz of shared amazement at this. I can see from their faces and the energy rippling around our circle that I've hit an exposed nerve.

These yoga girls, hardcore troublemakers that they are, are not seekers per se, not yet, at least. They're more often thrill-seekers, and self-abuse addicts, but a few, like Kali/Katy, Durga/Alex, and now Matrika/Molly, have become seekers-in-the-bud. And let's be real, in lockup most inmates are quite content to just get through the day without getting killed, or raped or beaten. Sure, they'd prefer to be on the Outs, having a smoke, snort or a drink, some nice groovy bump-and-grind, or going to a raunchy movie or a ganja-fogged rap jam, or an Ecstasy-laced rave. I'm not naïve. I know lots of girls come to class just to pass the time, wanting nothing more than to resume the life they've always lived once they get out. It's hard work to alter lifelong patterns. But while they're here with me they can hear about the choices I made, theirs to make, too—if they ever want to taste true happiness.

"The pay-off from doing mindful exercises," I say, "is learning to get in touch with our inner Self, with a capital S. Our true Self is the inner 'I'."

"But how we get to stay in that inner place, Miss?" Alicia, another new girl, asks, "after we do this lung-breathing?"

I say, "The easiest and best way is to always remember the Golden Rule: Do unto others as you want them to do unto you."

"I know that!" Alicia says. "My mama and gramma talks about that all the time."

"They are great caretakers and nurturers, as I'm sure most of your mamas and grammas mean to be. They teach you about kindness in many forms you don't notice are meaningful. Like the food we eat or substances we should or shouldn't put into our bodies. To embrace our inner *'I'* means being thoughtful and respectful of ourselves first, making it easier to express kindness to others. Every other person is a reflection of our own true Self. Those of you who keep coming to yoga class become more joyful. Why? Well, it's like Alex wrote in our class journal."

"You mean Durga," Alex interjects, in a soft voice.

"Sorry, yes, I mean Durga wrote this." I open the book and read aloud from Yoga Thoughts. "'Doing yoga has opened my heart. I now feel what it means to be happy for the first time since I was real little.'"

The circle is quiet. I look around at the girls who are dreamily reflecting on what I've just shared.

None of us on this day, months earlier, knew that not just one but a whole series of hurricanes would soon be in various stages of formation out in the breeding ground for such storms, the warm Atlantic waters off Africa's West Coast.

"Open heart, open mind," Kali says, repeating what she's heard me say many times.

Together now, we feel the vibration in our heart as we sing *Om*, the sound of the Eternal. Sometimes I have to remind the girls. "Find a sweeter, gentler sound," I suggest after a disturbing first round. "One a little less aggressive." Our second *Om* is a much nicer, more inviting, deeply massaging sound that soothes all our sore spots inside and out. "It's more like honey," I gently suggest. Our last *Om* gently cradles our hearts, opening us to the wellspring within.

Ready to do our kick-ass practice now, we stand, and soon the sweat begins to flow. "Misting," as Kali calls it, struggling and suffering in her hot polyester uniform.

CHAPTER 21

why? why not?

"So why d'you want to teach us?" the girls ask. I usually respond, "Because I'm just like you! And, starting with being sober, yoga helped me more than anything to turn my bad habits into better ones. That's why I want to share with you what works. But remember—it all starts with *the desire to improve our lives*."

At ABG I could let my guard down, not like in my own social milieu, and thus I revealed my well-kept secret. "What compels me to reach out to you guys is my own stepdaughter, Kara. She doesn't want anything to do with me. That's the truth. And believe me, it hurts to even say it."

But after speaking it aloud, I realized I had given it too much energy. I knew if I continued giving voice to it, the schism would completely tear me apart. So I decided to play down this sad fact in my private life. In yogic philosophy, we call deciding between several options, "practicing discrimination," or *viveka*. I decided to not dwell on the negatives. I realized I couldn't change my stepdaughter's teenage rejection of my up-till-then-welcome expressions of love. All I could change was my own attitude toward her. This is how I came to accept *what is*, being in a difficult home situation.

One day I casually revealed the source of my domestic difficulty. The girls reacted immediately. "Oh Miss, I'm so sorry, that's terrible," sad voices said in unison. "How come?"

I took a deep breath. Okay, I'd opened this can of worms, now I'd have to close it, but also let the girls know I'm human, that I can hurt as much as they do.

"Because her birth-mom hates me," I said as kindly as possible. "This poor woman lost the right to raise her own daughter. Imagine her pain. And I guess Kara, for whom I've been her day-to-day mom the past seven years—now wants to feel closer to her bio-mom. Most daughters rebel against their mothers, so maybe it's because I'm the main mother figure in Kara's life that she chose me to be shitty to. Lucky me. Until just recently, Kara and I were as close as you could imagine two females being, blood-related or not. Sometimes tragedy leads us to better things, you see? Her rejection drove me to seek you guys out! And look, we're having a great time, aren't we? Stepparenting sucks, but I had to do it. Many stepparents have to suffer their stepchildren's rejection, sooner or later. My case is textbook common. Luckily, from my personal heartache you've been able to learn all I ever wanted to share with my disinterested daughter.

"Such is the mysterious flow of life," I said, "and why we follow it. What we might perceive as *bad* sometimes turns out to be *the best*, in the long run. Of course, when we're struggling, it's impossible to see the positive results of the negatives, the hurts, the life-storms.

"Things always work out when we allow ourselves to *be* in the flow of life, and not resist what *is*."

CHAPTER 22

core strength

One day I speak of how important "faking it till you make it" is. I used this uplifting tool for practicing being positive and making better choices, as I set out to recover from my negative addictions.

"When bad things happen—either of our own making or due to some other circumstance that affects us—it's crucial to *fake accepting it*. Then we've let go of control. Only then can we stay in the center of our inner power.

"We do this when we've consciously chosen to be content."

When the girls arrive at the academy their inner Selves are in total disorder. All they know is how to live in fear. Ursula tells them in individual counseling sessions that their time there is "to instill positive new habits in place of your former bad choices. Habits don't die easily. The best way to change is to get new positive habits going, and the old ones just dissolve, painlessly."

Coming to yoga class separates the girls who are willing to improve themselves from those not interested in changing. Sha'ria and Lashanda, two warring gang girls, had been sent away from yoga class for unruliness, but at next week's class, Sha'ria returned. She asked for a yoga name and chose Maya (*the illusion of the world*). This was a sign of willingness for any girl, when she proudly asked for and chose her own yoga name.

Good-natured Ursula shows up in class one day. She asks for and chooses Leela (*the playfulness of the Divine*) as her yoga name, to show the girls she approves of our in-class rituals. She gives a smile and a wink to the girls next to her, so pleased to be sitting with the popular director in our circle.

"Miss Ursula is a yoga girl!" some murmur, awed by her addition to our group. Bigwigs and small fry, all of us, in one big circle. With each meeting we become more powerful, more comfortable with our inner wisdom, the center of our true reality.

Mr. Lawrence, in his slouched-over, uninterested manner, grumbles about all this "stupid name-changing," as he puts his walkie-talkie closer to his ear so he can't hear either the pleasantries or hardships discussed in our opening circle.

Later, Ursula pulls me aside as I'm leaving the building to return home after teaching my second class. "Even if only one girl is positively affected, your doing yoga with them is worth it. The yoga classes have brought a real sense of peacefulness to our entire community. Respect is creeping in where before there was none," she says, always encouraging me just when I need it. Sometimes it's lonely, spreading positive thinking to counterbalance the anger, hostility, and fear so rampant in today's world.

"Well, you got me babe," I joked. "And lots more like us."

"It's true, I know," Ursula said. "It's just so frustrating trying to make positive change within the system itself."

"And thanks, Ursula, for doing that," I say to this remarkable woman who's become a close friend. "When I arrived today, I witnessed another takedown. It really bummed me out to see it was Olga, a new regular. Old habits die hard, don't they?"

Ursula and I stood in silence for a moment, breathing as one, sharing the frustration as well as the joy of our similar passion. Both of us know how very hard it is to change, because we ourselves had to do it, each in our own way.

For me, everything changed when I decided to put down my former life as a confirmed bad girl, doing whatever I could to self-destruct before age twenty-one. For Ursula, she had to change the minds of others when she presented her unique approach to juvie reform, which the academy has now successfully proven. Both of us have worked hard for what we want. We knew most of these girls were lazy by nature. But the few that weren't—those who kept gravitating to the yoga class each week—had a chance to transform their lives, if they stayed positive, and didn't let negatives rule them.

"Yes, it's shocking," Ursula said in our sweet moment together, "to see how feeling bad can be so addictive. I'm sorry Olga forgot her inner *'I'* today."

"In class she's Maya," I said. "Isn't that ironic. That Sanskrit word means *the outer world is merely an illusion.*"

Ursula nodded. "Old ways are sure hard to change."

It's Charley's Friday now.

The ABG girls are worried for their families, as Ursula is, in St. Pete, worried about them. Anyone in the path of the storm faces impending danger. The last cell tower must have fallen, because there's been no word from Ursula or anyone else from the outside world for the last half hour. Curiously, the girls aren't worried about themselves, but others. Behind their hard exteriors, their hearts beat with love like all of ours do; even the worst of us has some compassion. Ever since the storm changed direction so suddenly, when it came far south of its originally predicted Tampa landfall, the girls have been more concerned about their families scattered all over the state of Florida than they are for their own safety.

Miss Estelle has done a good job of dispelling their fears. "This here building is like a fort made of steel n' brick," she's been telling them since they woke up to this sudden new reality: that the biggest, baddest storm they've ever heard of—is headed directly for little ol' Bowling Green.

Since it started plundering the region, Charley has stayed on its inland course, slowly moving in a northeasterly direction, following the Peace River corridor. As it churns ever more deeply into the land mass, it knocks over anything not cement or stone, at war with everything movable in its path.

Charley's eye—that core of dead-calm pussycat wind, the mind-tricking peace of its nucleus—is the storm's axis, its center. Outside that center, is hell. But within that innermost core—the storm's eye—is sublime peace.

Such is the similarity between our own lives and all of Nature. It's always safe for humans when we stay protected, deep in our inner-core sanctuary. In a hurricane, that place had better be in a brick or cement building. In our life, our center is our inner strength. As the girls have practiced, they know they can survive the worst of life-storms when they trust their inner truth, their inner *'I'*.

Charley's eye has traveled only a sluggish short distance across Florida's hot peninsula by the time it finishes tormenting the tiny hamlet of Nocatee. The storm, so massive, so slowly forward moving, bites deeply, screws relentlessly into the landscape like monster chopper-blades. It's only been on Florida's continental land shelf less than half an hour when the NHC announced it had already caused billions of dollars of destruction, from Port Charlotte up to the now-wasted town of Nocatee. Everything is flooded and torn apart in between. And still, it carves out its forward onslaught, heading straight to bludgeon scrawny Bowling Green.

Right toward my beautiful, incarcerated young souls. Their hearts shine strong, like beacons to me as I think of them from my safe haven-home in Lackland. From where it first struck Port Charlotte, north to Desoto County's town of Nocatee, 25-miles but nearly three hurricane-hours away—everything lies in helter-skelter shambles.

There's no peace on Florida's Peace River today. There's no political, class or cultural war going on, no immigration crush, no religious differences, no social unrest to equal that of this current nightmarish horror unleashed by Nature. Because when the weather decides to show you who's boss—there's nothing else to do but stay in the center of calm within, or face dire consequences. Stay in the safety of your being, the *'I'*—or risk being frightened to death. It's as simple as that.

CHAPTER 23

in the flow

Charley's sky-high monster eye looks like an alien peephole in images made from the space station, orbiting the Earth 150 miles overhead. Seen from much farther away satellite photos, the center appears as a giant black dot of a cosmic eye hovering miles above the Earth's swirling opaque cloud cover. On the ground, imperceptible to space imagery, the storm crawls forward like a waterlogged snail. The bull's-eye center is now striking the next center of civilization, five miles up the Peace River from Nocatee. Arcadia is an out-of-time cowboy-and-rodeo town, but right now it's suspended in a giant mixer, flooded, wind-whipped, and deserted. The town is absent its roughneck human inhabitants, as is every other place that Charley has trampled these last tense ninety minutes since invading the Sunshine State.

Quickly flattening the landscape in all directions, like a humongous plate of chop suey—organic vegetation and manmade materials, everything diced, disappeared and scattered—Charley demolishes Arcadia. Hugging the Peace River shoreline, it decimates in quick succession the smaller Brownville, then the miniscule, one-crossroads-blink called Limestone. The eye leaves behind any unprotected livestock drowned or nearly dead, or badly injured from flying sheet metal. The few terrified, holed-up humans sink into the comfort of prayer, their only hope, as they listen to their roofs lifting off the rafters.

There's always the rare person who refuses to leave their house, despite the mandatory evacuation notice in effect for hours beforehand. The National Guard does its best to rout out anyone not following orders. But there are always isolated individuals, afraid they'll lose their possessions from looters, too ignorant to realize they might lose their own lives if they don't leave. There's nothing you can say to such people, to open their shut-tight minds. They choose to stay and suffer the risks of facing a ferocious monster instead of running from it. Thrill seekers? Perhaps. Foolishly stubborn, more like it. Deaths always occur in instances where folks end up playing Russian roulette with Nature's unimaginable force of destruction.

Sometimes, for legitimate reasons, they stay. During Hurricane Andrew, the Category 5 system that caused extensive damage to metropolitan Miami in 1992, friends of mine were among the rare humans who chose to go through that deadly storm when they could have run the other way. The wife, for reasons unknown to any but them, chose to remain and safeguard her house from looters after the hurricane changed direction. It was headed right toward her home while her husband was away on a business trip. He flew to the airport closest to Miami and rented a car, practically the only vehicle on the highway into Coconut Grove, to join his terrified wife. Later, I heard their story.

"It was like standing next to a freight train all night, thinking the roof of the closet where we were hiding would cave in on us any second."

People do the oddest things when under stress.

"What's remarkable about that time," the husband later recalled, "was how people joined together in a united spirited way, afterwards. Instead of being afraid of looters, as we'd anticipated, and why we stayed home, all of those in our neighborhood gathered together like we'd never done before. We cooked food for each other. Everyone shared what drinking water or dry blankets we had with those who had none. Friends, families, and strangers alike shared generators and other necessities. I could hear the concert pianist who lived a couple houses away playing Brahms because there were no closed doors or windows, all were opened with no electricity. I had never heard him practice before this. Usually I can't hear anything over the AC blasting and all the windows closed."

It's true—when crises happen, people draw closer together.

When we share our fears and our joys, we're one big human family.

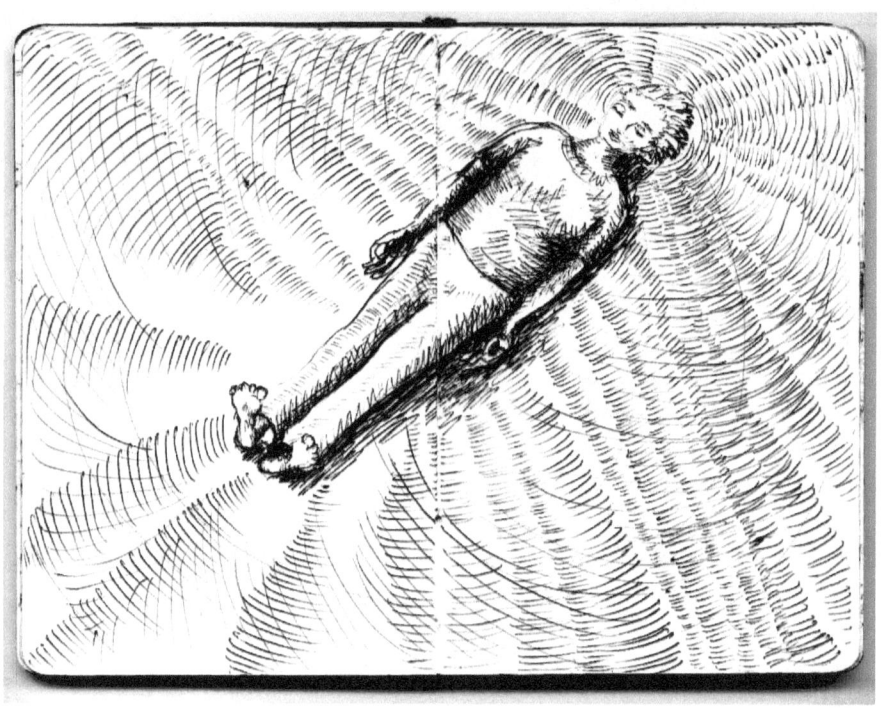

learning to access the Light within

CHAPTER 24

finding balance in
challenging times

C harley is now in its second hour pummeling small rural
counties of central Florida, famed for flat barrenness filled
with tens of thousands of acres of cattle and citrus groves.
The eye has just passed through Arcadia, 27 miles away from Port
Charlotte, where it began its land-grind. Coming straight up the Peace
River, the storm still heads directly for Bowling Green. Its core winds
haven't slowed down a bit, maintaining what was clocked at landfall,
147 mph. The powerful storm remains steady at Category 4 as it
inches toward my girls.

I'm at my house in Lackland, far from the academy. We've not
even lost electricity, with the storm's center well south of us now. We
listen to the weather channel talk about hurricane *fixes* that scientists
use to try to weaken a storm's destructive force. How planes fly close
to the eye when it's over ocean waters, to inject silver iodide from
spray jets. "Seeding a hurricane," it's called, but the announcer
admits it's unknown if this technique actually works. Other
experiments have been done before today. Like purposely spreading
large slicks of biodegradable oil over vast stretches of warm seas, in
hopes of dissipating a storm's intensity. And microwave satellites
aimed at storm centers, but if their concentrated frequencies lessen a

storm's ferocity, or if they work at all, again—there are no definitive answers.

As I watch I wonder if Estelle is sitting in front of the academy TV. I wonder if there's even power at the academy. I'm leaving the lines open and fight the urge to call Ursula.

I wonder how the girls are holding up, both those who take yoga and those not familiar with the state of the inner *'I'*.

Keeping the entire academy in my thoughts, I again go outside and stretch out my hands, sending protective energy to the two oak sentries guarding our home.

The last phone call between Ursula and Estelle, before tower service was lost, went something like this:

E: Miss Ursula, the regional supervisor Mr. Wayne, just called to check in.

U: I hope you told him what I said, the building is perfectly safe, and the girls ought to stay put like you and I agreed.

E: Well, Mr. Wayne, he still wonders if we should evacuate the girls to somewhere safer than here in Bowling Green. 'Cause it sure looks like Charley-eye be coming straight for us.

U: Yes, it does appear that way, Estelle. But our concrete building's the safest anywhere within fifty miles. I know from when I was shopping around for solid structures to convert into the program's facility. There's nowhere safer. Wayne doesn't know that, so I'll call him as soon as we hang up. How are the girls holding up?

E: Miss Ursula, you be proud of the girls. They not panicky one bit. Today a special day. Not one single takedown. Not a one. That almost a miracle, wouldn't you say?

Ursula agrees. Then she repeats for emphasis: Estelle, I've thought it through before calling you just now. I've definitely decided you and the girls need to stay put. I know others might tell you otherwise, maybe even the Police or the National Guard. But I'm taking full responsibility here. Don't go. Don't leave that building.

Tell them I've ordered you to stay and you have to obey me over the authorities. Okay?

E: Yes, Miss, I understand completely. I agrees with you. This here place ain't going nowhere.

U: Good. Just barricade yourselves best you can. In the cafeteria if the eye gets close to Bowling Green. All the girls and your whole staff can fit comfortably there. You can use the long dining tables to lie beneath if you need extra protection. Make them into an inside-structure you can crawl underneath if things really get bad.

E: Yes, Miss Ursula. I figured that what I do before you just said so, ah-huh.

U: Good. Stay put because that old building is the safest place in the entire county.

E: Yes'm, this place like Fort Knox.

U: You're so right, Estelle. Before we could get insurance as a correctional facility we had to replace the roof and hurricane-proof it, exchange all the glass windows with shatterproof Lexan, bulletproof plastic. We had to do a lot to convert that old building. Rafi and I were in charge of the renovation, so I know. I can guarantee how strong our structure is. I know its every beam, joist, wind tie-downs— the whole nine yards.

E: Well, I be. I never knew you was a construction person, too, Miss Ursula!

The two women laugh, two joyous souls shining in the face of adversity. Ursula is greatly relieved she's got Estelle on her team, especially during this emergency.

I'm home watching an oblivious tiny green lizard hop onto an oak tree trunk right in front of me. Even with the storm so close, the air is sometimes freakily almost-normal. We're in an expectant, gradual increase of wind. I'm sure the barometer must be pushing its limits. The air has the feeling of a pressure system trying to raise back-of-neck hairs. I remember how it's always like this just before every hurricane's ear-piercing shrieks begin. Hours of knock-down gusts precede a wet-devil blast—then the dead calm of a storm's eye—then several more hours of the back-end torment ... before the demon wind, lightning strikes, and rain taper down to ... normal.

I step closer to better see the lizard. I watch as its skin slowly turns from the bright green it was, fresh off a nearby leaf, to a brown that matches the bark it now stands on, completely unmindful of the storm approaching. The lizard hops onto an adjacent philodendron leaf, and its skin goes back to chartreuse. I wonder at the automatic adaptation it makes, and ask myself why we humans can't be as flexible as this lowly lizard? Some of us try, through whatever relationship we have with Great Spirit, the Mystery of All, Nature. Each of us is most fortified when we let our Big Heart within, our 'I' connect us to one another.

Adapting is necessary with buildings and humans, as well as lizards. Once upon a time the academy's original structure was a plantation house, or so Ursula was told by the locals who came for community events when the detention home for girls first opened. And at another time, the building was an earlier version of a private substance abuse treatment facility. In fact, during the renovation, Ursula and her team found old treatment records left behind from that era. There were decades-old musty 12-Step program literature and pamphlets in unused closets. Just before "The Dual Program" (as Ursula refers to her unique experiment) moved in, it'd been Elmer's Off the Beach, with that incomprehensible sign hanging outside, featuring a woman in a bikini beckoning customers to "Come On Inn," despite no beach within miles of Bowling Green. Several people in the community stopped to thank Ursula during ABG's construction days for taking the scantily clad woman down, the sign considered an eyesore by feminists and Baptists alike.

Once in conversation Ursula whispered, "There are secret passages throughout the building that few of the staff know about because we don't want the kids to make a run for it. Made us wonder if this building was used as a speakeasy during Prohibition, but nobody's been able to say. The deed says it was built in the early twenties. There was a closet at the end of one long hallway with a hatch beneath the floor and a staircase that led to an escape passage, a crude tunnel that came up a block away. I never went down there so can't tell you where it went. But it was an elaborate set-up, from what I was told. We sealed off the secret door, and put sheetrock over it during the renovation."

I'm thinking my life resembles a building that's gone through several incarnations of renovations like the academy, always evolving. I'd like to think my personal reconstruction project has bettered me, just as the beige and turquoise building that houses the girls is now a better place than it was as Elmer's Off the Beach, or a factory, or the speakeasy it may have been once. Just as Ursula used sheetrock and plaster, replacing rotten wood with new material, to better the old structure she chose to house her new special girls' program, I use tools of mindfulness to help uplift any person I can.

Whether we're talking about a person or a building, change brings choices. When I decided to transform my life, I sought help. When Ursula remodeled the old building, she hired experts. Sure, I hope the classes I teach the girls help make them better people. But I'll be happy if yoga just helps them get through the brunt of this damn storm rushing toward us right now.

Balance is a huge concept. To stand on one leg takes balance, and that is a great achievement for some. To stand on one's own power, and live without being controlled, or needing to control others in order to feel important—now that's a substantial show of a balancing act.

The many years of practicing yoga, learning to trust that deep inner rapport with the Mystery—the daily letting-go and letting-God, practicing life's balancing act—have brought me more happiness than I ever knew possible before. Now I accept life on its own terms. Before, I resisted, felt rejected and angry and saw myself as a victim. Such is the lot of the unbalanced life.

Even in hard times, challenges, and the inevitable adversity—I work hard to feel in tune, to stay in the flow, so now I get to enjoy a balanced life. No longer do I see life as a hardship or a curse, as I once did. I use my "fake it till I make it" mantra when stressed out, to stay connected to my inner *'I'*. Dang, repetition is the Mother of Learning!

Each time I get bumped off my center, my recovery time is shorter until I'm back within the calm *'I'* of that particular life-storm.

There's no big shake, epiphany or *a-ha!* about being aware and awake. Anyone can do it, if they wish to. Being anchored safely in the light-filled harbor of the inner *'I'* is a lot more fun than being tossed about by life's stormy calamities.

CHAPTER 25

prepare for the unexpected

ABG's anxiety-plagued girls didn't give a hoot about killer-storms, let's be honest. Moment-by-moment, their biggest concern was survival—being a bully or getting out of a worse bully's way. On Thursday they had no idea how awful things could become. But—by taking advantage of the distressful situation, I wanted to use the potential threat of deadly weather as a serendipitous teaching opportunity.

"Charley's eye, let's say, is a metaphor for your inner state," I said.

"A meta-who?" Cindy asked.

"A metaphor is a stand-in, to make something clearer. In this case, I'm using the killer-force of a hurricane, an *act of God* in insurance-speak, to illuminate what turmoil goes on inside us during disturbing times. Sometimes life feels like we're in an emotional upheaval, isn't that so?"

All heads nodded. Everyone knew exactly what I was talking about.

"When we feel in a state of dis-ease," I continued, "it's because we've given our power away. To someone or something else."

"Like some bully-girl, you mean, trying to stomp on my turf," Rene shouted. She was a gang girl recently sent to the academy from Tallahassee. The yoga name she chose was Viveka, *discrimination*.

Her gang tattoos ran all the way down the inside of her arm in a conspicuous *sleeve*, before that term was coined.

"That's right, Viveka. A choice, that's all it takes. The choice to change your entire life. That's the beginning of freedom from being controlled by others, or thinking you need to control, to be content with how things are. Sometimes life is scary, period. Just like Charley coming at us with maximum hurricane strength. If we can't let go of needing everything to be exactly the way we *think it* should be, our lives become one big agony of misery. Who wants that?"

All heads shake No!

"When we give up the need for control in our lives, then we begin to trust our inner guide. This is the reason we meditate in class. Learning to access the Light within, is why we do yoga exercises. So we can shut off the noise in our heads, and be able to feel, see, listen, and be guided by this all-knowing consciousness, within us. Spirit is within each human being, every animal and plant, and every thing in existence. In yoga, the air we breathe is also called the Light of consciousness, *prana*."

"What light?" Shay, with the wondrously allegorical name asked. Scrunched-up brows betrayed ShakespearesDelight's complete bafflement. "I never get this Light stuff. What's she talkin' 'bout?"

As usual, I let my students take over. By urging them to tap into the *Gee-You-Are-You* aspect of yoga, deep within, where the girls discover their inner guru, the inner teacher—I know they can shut off the extraneous BS of being human just as I had. When the girls learn to tap this infinite source of peace and calm and wisdom—by stilling their breath, experiencing the deep stillness within—they get hooked. No drug, no elixir, no sex-binge comes near to the thrill of experiencing the Light of Oneness. The regular girls now know this, intimately, comfortably. Their minds have experienced the quieting of their former freight-train brains. They've come to trust the inner 'I'.

"The Light is what makes us feel good about doing yoga, Shay," Julia answered.

"The Light, to me, is happiness," Maya says.

"It beats getting' high, doin' pills, or nursin' a bad-news hangover," said Kali. "Plus when we breathe right, y'know, lookin' at the Ins and Outs like Missy T here says, there's always this big bling-Light shining inside my head."

I laughed. The girls always think their brains getting more oxygen is tantamount to a new designer drug. A new girl always asks, "What's this light inside my head!" when she firsts learns to do diaphragm deep-breathing.

Then I explain it's the same technique used in sports, singing, and childbirth, three things these girls can relate to. "Those lights are more oxygen than you've ever experienced before! Isn't it amazing how shallow you've been breathing all your life?

"Yes," I say, "the Light we're talking about is more than oxygen. It's your deepest core of Being. It's being aware. Awareness has no limitations."

I look around. Every girl is listening, sitting up straight. No one's fooling around. Everyone sits like a stone, as if we are within a circle of protection, finding our way out of a labyrinth right there in our very own souls. The expectant faces wait to hear more. My heart bursts with pride over these yoga girls who've already learned to find answers to so many questions within themselves, by getting to know their own inner Self.

I said, "This Light within we speak of, appears when we quiet our monkey-mind. The Light is within us all, every single one of us. Even the baddest, dumbest, most unlikely. Anyone who hasn't yet tapped their inner Light, doesn't want to, doesn't believe it exists, or ... they're not patient enough to train their irascible monkey-mind."

"Say wha'?" Viveka yelps. "Irra- what? What monkey? In my head? What you talkin' 'bout now, Miss T?" Pale, pink, and dark-skinned gang girls all laugh good-naturedly at the new girl's shock.

Everyone else is used to the strange, out-there imagery we employ in yoga class.

Shay jumps in, "Monkey-mind is all that rapping inside our heads," she nods her head, "like Tupac on speakers 24/7."

Trinity shouts a jubilant sing-song "My homey!"

Others murmured, "Yeahh," nodding solemnly. I look around, noting these girls' adoring enthusiasm for a celebrity thug. So many things excite them about life, and we share them all in class. They love my spiritual approach, and I'm intrigued by their urban tribalism. They reap the reward of learning about inner spirit-work and I, likewise, expand my awareness by vicariously experiencing the thrills of their primal music and simulated-sex dance moves. Each time we meet we trade: I give them more Light and they share their angsty mistrust and fear. Unfortunately, that is all they've ever known.

For these girls, the truth of their life has been—and always will be, if they don't decide to change—to get laid, get high, and act out. They know *nada* about love, only sex, because they haven't yet learned to love themselves. Sex for these girls is about controlling another person, or another person controlling them. Lust might be the activator, but the end result for these young women is unhealthy attachment, Ursula had explained this to me much earlier.

"All relationships these girls know, is about codependency to the nth-degree. Each is so thirsty for love. Their hearts ache from the disadvantaged home lives they all have. But they need to start with Self-love. And that's what we teach them in every class they attend here at the academy."

At first, getting calm and getting centered seemed to each new girl ... well, boring. But after that first deep-breathing session at their first opening circle, they begin to sense the Light within themselves. Inside their cranial skulls, a light appears immediately, the result of true oxygenation for the first time in their lives. This Light inside their heads gets their attention. Then they begin to realize how amazingly free, easy, and light-hearted they now feel.

I tell them, "That's the first stage of en-*light*-enment." From that moment on, "the Light" never sounds dumb or unattainable, ever again.

Let's be real. When a girl first comes to class, "spiritual" means nothing more than spooks and ghosts to her, like those of Halloween.

Again, it's the Thursday before Charley.

As we complete a simple torso-twist on the floor, I offer another tidbit of grace.

"I'm here to show you guys how to feel good about just *being yourself*. You're much more than what you think you are. Mind-body-spirit, we're all three in one. That's what you really are, not just the stuff you see on the outside, the things called *ordinary*."

I look around; everyone's engaged in achieving their pose. I think, good, I have a captive audience. So I continue talking.

"Inside all of us is something extra-ordinary. That's our inner Self, with a big S. That special part of us is connected to our breath, and breath is connected to consciousness. If we're not breathing— we're dead, right? All this breath stuff means—it's not really complicated—is that we are One with everything, through our breath-consciousness."

The girls begin to unwind from one pose. I said we'd now go into a plank pose.

"Try counting silently to whatever number you want to hold this plank as your personal best. Remember it for next time we do plank."

I encourage each girl to be her own instructor. "Once you know where to put your limbs, and remember to breathe correctly—your body becomes your best teacher, ever!"

"What chou talkin' 'bout now, Miss?" Kali wails as she falls out of plank, laughing. "You always throwin' stuff at us when we supposed to be concentratin'."

I laugh. "Yeah, I love it when I have your full attention. And you know how much effort it takes to do a pose like side twist. So, let's do that next, shall we? Wow, you guys are awesome!"

Later, we're taking a short break before our next pose, a triangle.

"So what's this about that Light stuff, again?" Viveka asks. She's still adjusting to the unusual things we do and talk about, here in yoga class.

As the girls sit and rest from their varying degrees of effort, readying themselves for the next pose, I explain, "There's more than fireworks going off in your brains when you take a deep breath of air, that's for sure. I mean those feelings the Light shines on, inside, the ones that tell you there's more to living than just getting high, getting laid, getting in or out of trouble. Those whispers you get—you know what I mean, we all have them—telling us there's something more going on here than what appears to be. And that whispering, your inner *'I'* speaking, is an important key to figuring out who you really are."

Kali, who always has something useful to offer, pipes up, "But how can we believe something we can't see?"

"Good question, Kali. That's what everyone asks, people of all beliefs. In yoga we learn to be happy from the inside out, and you *feel* that's true each time we do a pose. Anybody know why?"

I pause and look around.

Alice, a striking blonde who shockingly looks like she belongs in an Ivy League prep school, not a reform school, says, "Because we're stilling our minds. And allowing the bigger mind of the Universe to shine within us."

"Awesome, Alice. You rock!" I say. "Anyone else?"

French Fry offers, "Well, when I'm workin' hard at these exercises I'm happy, just knowin' I can do somethin' so hard. And that gives me esteem."

"Yes!" I exclaim. "You're so right, French Fry. Remember when you first came? You kept saying, 'I can't do this!'"

"Yeah," she answers, "and you told us that's a negative mantra. You said we have to start sayin', 'I can do it!' And you were right, Miss T! I'm doin' it. I never thought I could do these freaky pretzel poses, ever! Not in a thousand years!"

Everyone mumbles their agreement. They've all been called out by me for saying "I can't do it." No one is allowed to say these words in class without suffering the consequence of me demonstrating how that's a negative mantra. "Instead of saying 'I can't,' we start by faking it till we make it. So … for any new direction we want to go in, any new thing we want to do, we say to ourselves, 'I can do this!'"

Then the class goes into a standing head-to-knee stretch, following my step-by-step instructions. Breathing deeply, in silence, listening to their breath. Going deeper in the stretch with each breath. Feeling their bodies release tension. Focusing their eyes on one spot on the soiled rug we worked on. I ease the girls back after a nice long stretch on one side. We then do the other side, to balance our bodies. To calm our minds. To strengthen our spirits.

Again, we sit in silence in our spread-out fashion across the large common room. In the corner glisten a few pieces of glass from the girls' community altar. I look more closely and wonder who's added the elastic tie with a few strands of hair still wrapped around it, and why. Anything and everything is considered sacred and worthy for this altar at the academy.

I softly ask, "Anybody here feel a little better since they've been coming to yoga class?"

Everyone in the room, even Twinkie, last week's new girl, raises her hand. Kali looks around, almost gloating, in her senior position among the girls, at the newfound happiness yoga brings. I look at Twinkie's radiant face. It's as if a lightbulb has gone on, from the way she's lit up. The troubled look she arrived with earlier—gone.

"Oh, I get it now!" Twinkie says. "I feel good 'bout me cuz I just did a sun salute first try!"

"Excellent example," I say.

"So you mean if I feel happy, like I did last week when I could do a sun salute after a few tries, and just now, doing it right off like I done—that's proof I can be good, instead of doing the bad stuff I do like crank and screwing around?"

All the girls giggle at this. No one's supposed to mention drugs beyond the bounds of private counseling sessions, but yoga class is viewed as a Judgment-Free Zone. Ursula and I agreed to this from the start. "What goes on in your class, stays there," she told me, as a sign of trust. "I know you'll tell me if there's something inappropriate I need to address."

I nod my head at what Twinkie just said. "Yeah, that's about it. It's pretty simple. To change, all we have to do is make that choice. It helps to have a teacher to remind us of what we've learned. But if you don't, there are plenty of books out there. I learned to do yoga from a book. But for meditation, I needed a teacher, to go deep."

"Really?" Kali sounds astounded. She's never heard me mention this before.

"Wow, you make meditation sound so easy, Miss T," Twinkie says.

"It is," I answer.

"Learn to *Be* with who you really are, the real you," I say. "We're learning to stay in the core of our being, in class. We get there, almost like on a bridge crossing from one part of ourselves to another, higher, more fun part—by focusing on our breath. The key is the breath. If you learn nothing else here, your life will change if you remember to watch your breath as it slowly comes in ... and watch it slowly leave."

"I can do that!" Twinkie says. Nods and loud agreements follow from all the other girls, who are ready for our final pose of the class.

"Let's stand and do a tree, a one-legged balancing pose, shall we?" Everyone loves the tree. The regulars are quite good at it. The newer girls hug a wall for extra support. We stand with our feet firmly anchored, our limbs articulated, our spines stretching like an invisible puppet master is pulling us up by strings attached to the top of our skulls. Tall, proud, wonderful girl-mountains—with a tree on top. A whole room of us.

We slowly unwind from standing on one leg, then engage every muscle it takes to stand in balance on the other. Our eyes focus on a precise spot on the carpet. Our breathing is deep, natural, making the ocean-sound. We are in the yoga groove. Totally.

Slowly we loosen our limbs and I say, "Now for your favorite pose."

"Savasana!" They all shout in unison.

I laugh. "That's right, meditation time, girls. Time to go within, to know the real you, the eternal Spirit that lives inside, wearing this outside garment called *your life*. Let's enter our own body-temple now, and ... follow our breath ... in ... watch our breath ... as it leaves ... out ... then, breathing in ..."

The room becomes silent. From a far-off place in the academy, we hear the mumbling of voices. Mr. Lawrence's walkie-talkie, in his crumpled spot in the far corner, cheeps like a melancholic bird in a tree of its own, right there close to us. As we connect with this place within ourselves, we connect with All that is.

"This place, this Light," I softly say, "protects us ... shows us our true Source ... guides us ... whenever we ask ... we receive ... watch this inner place ... see the Light ... of your breath illuminate all there is ... all that will be ... all that was ... is Oneness ...."

I meditate sitting up while the girls lie on institutional carpet all around me. I'm surrounded by a garden of wonderful beings. Peaceful "bad" girls who want nothing more than to know the good within them.

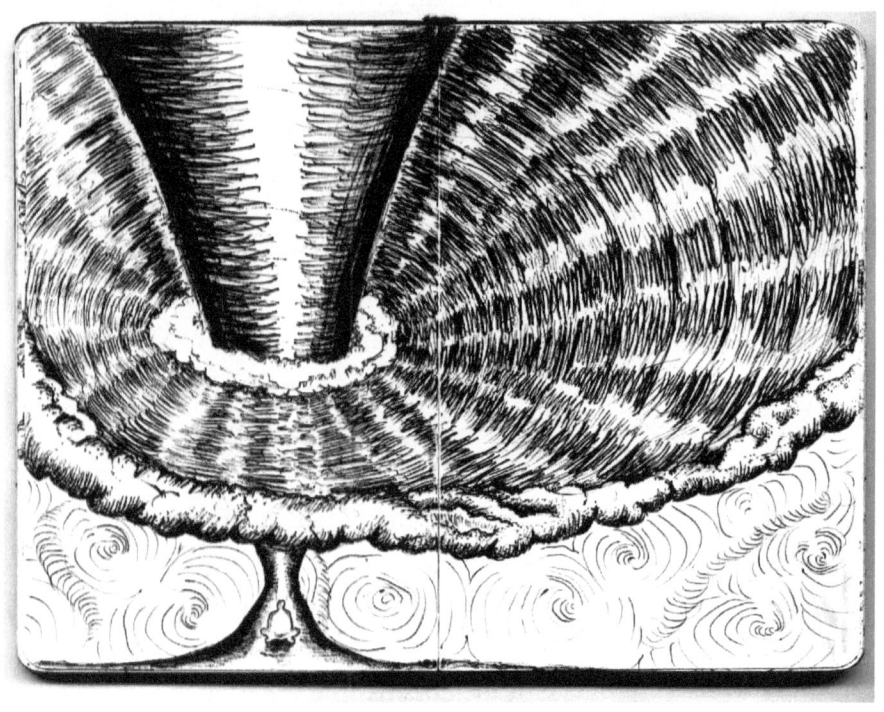

staying in the core, the 'I' within, through all of life's ups and downs

CHAPTER 26

the light is sometimes
a shadow

Charley's rampage is in its third hour. The system has just ravaged tiny Limestone and is currently slaughtering the speck that is Ona, more like *Oh No!* to the terrified few who foolishly stayed behind. The storm has blown off roofs of scattered trailers and unsafe dwellings that now lay in shambles, scattered among thousands of acres of orange groves and cattle pastures all over the countryside.

Charley's eye has again done its inexorable war dance. Unpredictably, it jumped two miles west from the Peace River basin, and mercilessly hit poor Ona dead-on, the place barely more than an intersection with only a dimly lit store no bigger than a hut (which sadly, is no more), where people used to buy their bread and milk. The other life-necessity thereabouts, beer, had to be found over the county line as this confirmed Baptist county is dry as a bone, liquor-wise. It's the same county where Elmer's Off the Beach, the former establishment at the academy site, served only Coke and GatorAid, and back in the Prohibition, the harder stuff (on the sly), when those tunnels were put to good use.

Hop, skip, and jump, in gigantic fashion, is what landlocked whirley-canes do, more than when they're traveling over open seas.

The eye of a storm is extremely, outlandishly and physically outward. A person's true nature, however, our innermost core—is exactly opposite. Our *'I'* is profoundly and lovingly, inward.

A person has to be conscious to make a choice. Choosing demands recognition in order to reach a decision. For the girls, their true potential—re-cognizing that peaceful center within—is their best bet to knowing Self-love. A hurricane, earthquake, tidal wave or wild fire—these forces of Nature have no choices to make. Huge displays of Nature's power just are. They simply exist.

We humans are the lucky ones. We have the power to decide how we want to exist: in fear of being controlled by outside forces, or in the free state of accepting life *as it is*, which is the definition of Self-love.

Charley's devilish strength is heading straight for Zolfo Springs, seven miles south of Bowling Green, where the girls are being gathered and lined up by Estelle and her staff. Soon, sixty-two people will be brought into the confines of the safest area of their fortress-like facility, the common room, where the girls and I do yoga each Thursday.

The academy's altar sparkles from the room's dark corner, sending out reminders of hope. An occasional token of gratitude gleams from the shelf right into the girls' hearts. Even if they forget to speak aloud words of comfort to each other, the symbolic tokens girls have placed on the altar speak for them.

From my house in Lackland I'm thinking of my girls. I know they're in safe hands. But I won't find out until a few days later that Ursula decided to stay with her family in St. Pete. Estelle and Lawrence and eight other staff are managing the girls today. As I sit waiting out the brunt of Charley's winds, glad that my family is not close to the pinpoint of the storm's nucleus, I remember how eager the girls have always been to learn all they could from me. Once they accepted how yoga empowered them, they began to release feeling fearful, and accepting more of what life is.

I recall a time, months earlier, during our opening circle. It was Lakendra, I believe, who asked *the* question.

"So how can we change? I really want to, but I get confused about making it happen."

I answered, "We're all learning how, right here." I look at the faces surrounding me. I sense their frustration. I know they want to experience the heights of joy available to them, not the snakepit their previous choices dragged them into. I inhale and dive in.

"Doing yoga is like developing spiritual *muscles* along with your physical ones. Little by little, we learn, experience by experience, how to stay in the Light. Yoga encourages the positives to grow stronger than the negatives in our spirits. We let the darkness of our life dissolve, melt away on its own, like a splinter that works its way out when it's ready. Each week you grow stronger, doing time doing yoga, and eventually—you become empowered. That way you can conquer the inner demons each of us has. These demons are called our *shadow selves*. Every person has them. It's as if we came into this world with a good side and a not-so-good side. Which side we let grow stronger, is up to us.

"As someone who had a whole truckload of demons that used to camp out inside me, within my monkey-mind I mean, I can guarantee you only one thing. The demons within leave you alone *only* if you do a workout that enlarges and empowers your good, Light-filled side. Like yoga, or prayer, or some other form of positive reinforcement."

I look around the circle and see I've got my girls hooked. Good. Now I'll give them the double-bait I only use for addicted-to-the-Dark sorts, like they are. Like I used to be. That's how I wound up here, after all.

"You'll never need to anesthetize yourself again," I say softly, "on drugs, acting-out, or any other bad choices, ever, if you encourage your spiritual muscles to get strong. Focus on taming your demons, confront them head-on, and your shadow-self will dissolve—that's how you'll be free. That's how to be victorious over the inner darkness, which the shadow-self is. We stop fighting the battle of good vs. bad, which is what addictions are: both bad and good ones. We don't fight the bad ones simply by 'seeing' what's bad for us, just for us, and not doing it anymore. And immediately substituting a good addiction, like exercise, or yoga, in the old destructive one's place. This giving up fighting, is true surrender. This is how you become a winner, not a loser."

"Wow," a girl nicknamed BowWow barked. "That's way cool! You really think I can learn to do that shit—oops, sorry!" Hoping not to get marked down for a critical, BowWow looked sheepishly over at Mr. Lawrence huddled in the corner, pretending he didn't notice the profanity, a punishable offense.

"Sure. All of you can," I reply, brushing over the gaffe. Giving no attention to this infringement of the academy's guidelines, we move on. I figure that those who've found their way to yoga class have had little, if any, exposure to the inner 'I' in their spiritually impoverished lives.

"The path to happiness isn't a straight line. All of us on the spiritual path take a step forward, then a few backward, then a couple more forward, then more back slides, a regular do-se-do until finally—one fine day—we wake up and instead of a millisecond of happiness, we actually feel all right for, oh, maybe five minutes. Then we practice meditation and hold some more poses, and our happiness factor stretches into more minutes, a half-hour, a couple hours, until we wake up to find that we went through an entire day feeling life is ... just okay. The way it really is.

"Let's be honest. You're battling some pretty big demons here in lockup. You have high hurdles to jump over and believe me, I know how hard it is to let go of old habits. Each day you're learning more ways to fight off the fear and negative addictions that have gripped your soul hard. Don't be discouraged though, ever! Learn to let your inner Light shine."

"Yeaaaah," some of the girls say, expressing their dreams with longing. They're beginning to get the picture.

"Cool, dude," Lakeeshina whispered.

"The Light rocks!" Shay exclaimed.

"Start by accepting who you are, right here, right now," I urged. "And then forgive yourself, totally, for what you don't like about yourself. So let's stand and begin with a few sun salutes, shall we?"

I stood and the girls did too, smiling and squirming. About as focused as a bag of worms, yet willing to do the asanas they'd learned to anticipate each week.

As I sit waiting out Charley's bad manners to arrive on Friday, I recall a private conversation with Kali, my star pupil.

"I tried killing myself once," Kali nervously admitted, her eyes darting around to ensure no one else heard her, although anyone could have figured this out. Kali stared at the scars on both her wrists. "But I feel stronger now."

"The nearest I came to losing my life," my whisper matched Kali's, "was when a jilted boyfriend of mine tried to kill me. He took us out on a boat and threw me overboard and held my head underwater. But I managed to break free. We were both on drugs. It was a product of how much I liked danger back then. I guess I was addicted to being bad. Maybe my mom called me a *bad girl* once too often and I started believing it. This boyfriend, well, when you hang with people who let fear rule their lives, they're not in their *right minds*. Checking-out with booze or drugs, murder or suicide, self-loathing, intolerance—that was me before I learned to embrace my true nature."

"Your true nature?"

"Yes, Kali, the same one you have, the deep you. The one that knows your essence is pure Love."

Kali's eyes grew rounder. "Yes, I've felt it sometimes," she murmured.

"I think," I quietly admitted, "I wanted that guy to do what I didn't have the guts to do. Like you did."

Kali absorbed this in silence.

"Just like you," I said, "I was trying to kill myself, back then. My weapons of spiritual destruction were substance abuse and inappropriate relationships. Plus that boyfriend of mine, who nearly succeeded in doing what I'd put him in my life to do."

Kali blinked slowly, hearing my story. My death-by-association suicide attempt. She asked in a low voice. "Did it change you, Miss?"

I also lowered my voice for the shared confession. "It made me realize that every choice I make counts. Even having a loser-boyfriend, which I thought at the time was just for fun. But he could easily have killed me that day. Too easily."

Kali wanted to talk more so she stood quietly by my side as Mr. Lawrence herded the girls out of the room to the next classes. She asked in a calm but desperate tone: "So what about when I don't believe all this stuff you tell us? Sometimes I can't help thinking you make it all up, that you're lying to us."

I hold her honest gaze steadily in mine, knowing full well that Kali was one of a handful of girls experiencing a real spiritual breakthrough, right there in lockup. Her progress from angry arrogance, humiliated absconder, back to supercilious defiance had been a series of masks she'd worn. But her true self is the smiling, curious soul I have grown to love, beneath that tough outer shell of hers. Kali's longing for liberation, true soul-freedom, was that of my own, so many years before. To come from such hardship and self-loathing, to cultivating a closeness with her spiritual side, even here in prison, impressed me.

"If that's how you feel, you have to work through your doubts yourself, Kali. It's called self-inquiry. You know how, I've shown you. People have to base how much they trust the power within on their own personal experiences. Think about what makes you keep coming back to yoga class. It feels good, right? Your body has grown stronger. You're learning to calm that monkey-mind of yours with breath work. And now you're practically an expert in tapping the energy we connect with, through meditation. Each time you practice all these yogic techniques, you're going deeper within. Familiarizing yourself with that inner power through your breath and the poses, like opening gates within you, all this stills your addicted-to-busy mind. Everything adds up when you continue the process of self-inquiry. Just keep doing yoga, especially on the Outs when you're released.

"You're beginning to have extra-sensory experiences, the inner adventures of the spirit. The world within is infinite in possibilities. First you learned to trust me, your teacher, and now you're starting to trust yourself, the guru within. And you're now having real experiences to base that trust on. Your experiences, one by one, show you the way to freedom, even while you're doing time here."

The line of girls was almost out the door. Mr. Lawrence looked nervously over at Kali and me, so I arched my brows to acknowledge his concern. "She'll be right with you, sir," I said.

"Just one more thing before you go, Kali. A suggestion. Start asking that same question to your inner teacher, and see what comes up. Ask, 'Why should I trust my inner Self?' Get quiet and really listen. You have all the answers inside, Kali. You're finally learning to love yourself. Your 'I' is in the infant stage, so don't beat yourself up. The truth will appear if you want to know it. It'll happen, but only when you're ready. If you wish to be happy, stay focused on your inner strength. Everything will come to you that you need, so you can experience that connection to the real you. It's the joy of Self-love, which is the opposite of self-hatred, that drove both you and me to such extremes. But get ready. Those of us who've already been to hell, when we commit to cultivating Self-love, we go as high as heaven on earth; just you wait. You'll do it. I can tell."

"You can?" Kali's crystal clear blue eyes sparkled and her red hair seemed to burst like fireworks going off.

"Yes. You're curious about the truth, and so you'll find it, in your own time. Now you just need to practice the techniques you've learned. You're not stuck in self-doubt and self-hatred anymore, so be patient. Those horrible feelings were never yours, you know."

"They weren't? They felt like mine."

I'm walking with Kali now, whispering at her side as Mr. Lawrence leads the line of girls down the hall. We need to finish this conversation soon.

"Fear of the unknown is something you learned. Emotional pain is not a trait you were born with. Fear is created when things happen to us. Inside, in our pure state, there's nothing but pure joy."

"Really?"

"Really, Kali. So just keep doing the breath-work and mindful exercises like the poses, and you'll have more inner experiences that will show you what to do next. Circumstances will shift if you continue fanning this fire that yoga ignites inside you."

"Fire?" Her voice lifted. Whenever I spoke of this classic metaphor to describe the power born from doing yoga or other mindful practices, the girls were always curious to hear more. The awakening of consciousness centers, called chakras, is another way of describing this uplifting *fire* that is stimulated by a regular spiritual practice.

"The purifying energy of yoga is called *fire*, Kali. It's not real flames that burn, but an energy within you that unblocks fear, pain and all negativity—so you can discover who you are. The you that's connected to the source of joy, of bliss within us all."

"Oh." Kali was speechless. Even though she'd heard all this before, it always fascinated her.

Our heads were very close. None of the other girls in the line ahead of us, busy gossiping and teasing each other, were aware such a conversation was taking place a few feet from them. They were wondering what was for lunch, bemoaning the fact they can never shave their hairy legs there in lockup, worrying when they'll be allowed to call home.

We've reached the classroom door of her math class. I must part from Kali. I gently put my hand on her shoulder.

"Keep focused on your Big Heart, Kali, where the powerful energy of Spirit resides most strongly. Try to remember, as you work out any negative feelings like the doubt you tell me you have, that as much as you might *think* you doubt, or *think* you hate yourself, you'll one day learn it was only Love in disguise. You can't truly see the Light till you've known the Darkness. Trust me on this, Kali."

Her once-defiant eyes shone with a kindled brilliance I'd noticed there before. Kali's face beamed as if her inner beacon had just been lit.

"Really?" she whispered.

"Trust me," I repeat. "It happened to me; it'll happen to you, too, if you want that experience. True happiness can be yours. What happens is what you desire and seek; so focus on that. It's that simple."

I turned to go. Kali urgently grabbed my arm and drew closer, saying, "But Miss T, I have a problem." I faced her again and waited for her to explain. "How exactly do I deal with the demons?" she asked in a low, quivering voice.

"Confront them," I firmly stated. "Otherwise they'll keep returning, wearing different masks. Pretend those bad feelings of yours are like ugly beasts that live inside you, and you are their only master. Keep faking it, believing that you're *training them*. Pretend you're okay, that you're making these inner monsters of yours *behave!* They are your shadow-side, that's all. Pretty soon, you'll believe it. Your fears are imaginary demons that hide inside you. You can get them out of your head by commanding them to not bother you anymore. It takes practice, that's for sure. But keep telling them to leave and they will."

The other girls' talkative maelstrom erupted around us. I saw the math teacher looking at me as if to ask, *What's up?* I had to get out of this classroom.

"One last thing, and I really have to go, Kali. All of us have to witness whatever those demons are trying to show us, even if it's painful.

"Even when authorities do so-called terrible things to us, acting like demons themselves—such as the court system, or for others, whatever administration is in charge of the government—we must learn the spiritual lesson that's being offered. Never blame someone else for your own unhappiness.

"Listen to what they say to you," I whispered, nodding to the math teacher to indicate I was leaving. "Make better choices. Command those bastards out of your head every time they try to mess with you. Do it with courage, without getting high. You'll slay your inner dragons if you just keep trying. They do die away, trust me on this.

"It's the challenge all of us must meet—to conquer our dark side. We become the winner when we surrender to Self-love, and leave behind the fear these monsters really are. Be courageous and remember the centering tools: breathing, letting-go, your poses. Gradually, you'll learn to trust the inner wisdom that grows stronger within you daily, stronger than the dragon of addiction, stronger than the monkey-mind of brain chatter.

"Each time you harness breath with any activity, whether you're doing yoga or brushing your teeth—you'll know more about your inner Self. If you stay centered within, you can then be true to your higher Self. You'll be spiritually empowered. Your life becomes the fulfillment of your destiny, not just something that happens to you."

CHAPTER 27

the test

As Charley draws closer, I wonder if the girls are scared out of their wits, or ready to have the experience of a lifetime. I know Estelle and Lawrence and the other staff are taking good care of them, so I'm not worried. I'm sitting at my kitchen table drinking a cup of tea. The rest of my family is busy elsewhere waiting for the tail end of Charley to pass. My mind returns to previous events at the academy. The biggest crisis that Ursula and I had to face together, during my time with the girls, was over religion.

The trouble started a year after I'd been there, when fundamentalist Christian ladies started coming to hold Bible studies with the girls. Then—all fury broke loose.

"The lady told me I'd go to hell if I meditated," Sha'ron said to me when she showed up at our next yoga session.

"They say I can't believe that God is inside me! They told me I'd go to hell if I ever thought that," Reemie tossed out like a stink bomb into the middle of our opening circle.

"The ladies who come to do Bible study say you're into black magic," Theresa declared.

Amber meekly added, "I said I didn't agree with them and they got mad. And told me I was a sinner."

The other girls looked to me for clues. Two guilt-ridden Christian girls now presented a major enigma for our circle that day.

However it might appear to the contrary—I welcomed the opportunity to discuss this topic. Since moving to the Bible belt, I'd faced prejudice and ostracism and been personally attacked and vilified for my personal God-is-All belief. Lackland—where Will was living with his kids when we married, and where we were forced to stay because of his obligations—was the most evangelical Christian town I'd ever known. Since moving there I'd heard every reason imaginable for judgment against my approach to loving Spirit.

I clearly remembered our circle that day at ABG. Newly returned from her runaway theatrics, Kali sat with her arms folded over her chest, waiting to see how I'd handle this damning evidence presented by the frightened Christian girls. "The yoga teacher is corrupting you girls' souls," the evangelical volunteers warned.

Two girls who feared they'd go to hell if they continued doing yoga with me, were there only to tell me how angry they were that I'd been ruining their chances for heavenly salvation.

"You have no right, Miss!"

"Your way isn't our way!"

"They said you're into the occult. That yoga is Devil worship!"

"I'm here just to tell you I hate you!"

"I should never have trusted you. Look at me! Now I'm going to hell!"

The girls' anger shocked me. I was sucked into a strange state hearing this. Half of me was glad it finally was out of the closet, this *ism* against anything new or strange. With the social climate less than progressive in central Florida, I should have expected it. Now we were talking about what festered behind the facade of every cheery Christian I'd met since moving to the South. The other half of me felt like crying, because I loved these girls and I'd brought torment to them, just by wanting to teach them the joys of doing yoga. How do I approach this? I wondered that day.

I reminded myself that being angry is the girls' normal state. Having been fed religious dogma stating that their souls would be cast into hell if they practiced yoga or meditated, by well-meaning but misled people who took the Bible literally and used it to disparage anything unfamiliar to them—made all twelve girls more upset than I'd ever seen them before. Madder than they'd been over the State of Florida putting a stop to their partying and "freakin' with the bros in the hood." Everything they'd ever been angry at paled in comparison to this bomb going off in our circle of intention that day.

I pressed the space between my eyebrows. And took a deep breath.

I must defend mindful practices, I thought. I felt compelled to defend my own quest I'd had since adolescence, that led me to explore the spiritual itch I had, outside of my parents' and my culture's westernized Christianity.

I needed to defend myself, as someone who felt very surely that God is Oneness, experienced everywhere, in everything. It is my Truth. I didn't find relief for my spiritual itch in one particular religion or political party, or a conventional lifestyle either. I must try to paint the picture of equality. That all of us have the right to choose the life we want. I chose a different way from my parents. These girls before me may choose their parents' way, or they may find their own. The choice is for each of us to make. That's what I object to about religious proselytizers: people insisting their beliefs are the only truth.

My own questions about heaven, hell, sin, who am I *really*, what's good and what's bad—specific questions regarding my own Truth—I searched high and low for. The Bible of my upbringing did not provide answers for my quest, and the Church certainly didn't either. Only when I learned to meditate did I find, instantaneously— my own Truth. I felt compelled to defend all non-Christian philosophies, not for my sake, but because I've always admired all lovers of Spirit, in all forms. I didn't need every person I met to like my peculiar spiritual practices, chanting, meditating, doing rituals of intention. Yet I wanted to address the girls' uncertainty. I needed to defend yoga and the peace of mind it brings, with answers I knew the committed Christian girls were seeking right then, having just been told that what we did in yoga class was jeopardizing their very souls.

Since I moved to Lackland, strangers, usually women, had come right up to me and brazenly asked, "Have you taken Jesus as your personal savior?" So I'd had plenty of practice about what I was to say to my girls.

"Why yes," I'd always respond. Adding, incredulously, "Haven't you?"

To me, Jesus is a great soul, by far among the most important, alongside Buddha and Muhammad and more contemporary great teachers I've studied with. My answer always throws implacable fundamentalists off balance, those who believe they have all the right answers. "I call myself a spiritual warrior," I'll say to anyone who brings up God, whether their opinions come from Om of Vedanta, God of the Torah, Jesus of the Bible's New Testament, Allah of Muhammad's Koran, or … the Nature deity of that sacred tree over there.

⚜

Now I was addressing my conflicted circle of yoga students.

"Girls, do you know the biblical verse: '… your body is a temple of the Holy Spirit within you.' from 1 Corinthians 6? For me, I had to experience the inner power, for myself—which by the way, is just another name for the Holy Spirit—before I knew what those words in the Bible really meant. I've always liked the sound of calling myself *a spiritual warrior*, although these days I've refined my job description to *spiritual activist*. I'm a warrior, an activist for the simplest, highest-good kind of Truth. If anyone wants to criticize how I worship the Divine, they simply don't realize mine is exactly the same God as theirs. There is only one Source. There's only one God, but there are many names for It.

"So here today, in our circle, I'm speaking to you guys from my heart, not from some condemning control center. I don't judge. That's for pushy people, folks who try to ram *their* interpretation of Truth down other's throats. Anybody who says I'm not godly doesn't know me. I'm a true blue God-junkie who considers herself absolutely addicted to Him/Her/It, in all the many forms the sacred takes. To me, God is Life itself. God is All. God is—indescribable, really.

"I'm sorry, girls, you strict Christians especially, that you got a dose of the judgment those Christian ladies threw at you. Miss Ursula won't be pleased to hear about this. Those volunteers are well-meaning, no doubt, but still, what they said to you is deeply disturbing. And wrong. Somehow many religious people feel they must belittle others not of their faith, in their zeal for spreading what their particular brand of godliness means to them."

Now there was a rumbling in our circle. Upset faces. Angry curses under breaths. Daggered-glances thrown toward me. I waited for the girls to quiet down. Then I spoke softly from a place deep within. I took a deep breath.

"The word *God* has a different meaning for every person. Jesus Christ is a member of the God-head to many of us who were raised Christians, and to others who weren't, he is something entirely different. A Muslim told me that in the Koran, Mother Mary gets more attention than her son, Jesus.

"Names are tricky. That's why I prefer to use the word Spirit when talking about God. One of my teachers, a very wise, ninety-ish Christian monk, once told me, 'Everyone has their own interpretation of what the name God means.' So he taught us to use the designation Spirit, instead of God, to speak of this Mystery.

"Spirit is at our very center. What we do here in class is not just what it says on paper: stress-reduction and self-empowerment, as Miss Ursula calls it. I call yoga *praying* with my body. I use my yoga practice like other people use religious rituals. But yoga is not a religion. It is an ancient, pre-Hindu philosophy. People of many religions practice yoga. I've studied with great Jewish, Christian, Hindu and Buddhist yoga and meditation guides whose teachings are based on various yogic texts, called scripture, exactly as the Torah, the Bible, and the Koran are."

I looked around the circle. The girls were spellbound, listening with rapt attention, even the worried religious ones. So I continued.

"Buddha was a yogi searching for Truth before he became enlightened. It was his followers who started calling themselves Buddhists, just like Jesus' followers came to call themselves Christians, and followers of Muhammad call themselves Muslims. All the world's great religions began with people searching for their Truth.

"Each of us can find God on our own. But usually this profound concept is passed down to us from our parents and our culture. The Truth, when we finally know it, always feels right within our Big Hearts. Some of us feel that awareness of God's Mystery on our own. Others never get to personally experience it, and they have to take the word of others that it exists. Until—something ignites our spiritual yearning, or some outside influence shows us—and we realize we are Spirit incarnate.

"We're all unique. For me, my parents' way of finding Truth just didn't answer those deep questions I had, starting in adolescence. I had to search my Truth out on my own.

"And what I found—the concept of Oneness, pure Love that I believe Truth is—through my asana practice, that led me to study Eastern thought, including scriptural sources, and practicing stilling the mind, works best in my life."

I looked over at Alex/Durga then and recalled how she'd written in our Yoga Thoughts journal, after having just started to come to class: "Yoga has made my head and my heart feel open, like a big flower inside me I never knew could be opened. I love yoga!"

Alex's eyes, dark pools of neediness, directed me now to what I had to say, for her sake. I knew the intense dread she felt, I knew about her being a former cutter. Fortified by Alex's love of yoga, I took a deep breath and dove in deeper:

"When you realize everything you need is right within you, your natural self—without outside stimulants—you become your own best teacher. You begin to embrace your own Light within."

Durga looked down at the floor, as I was sending my understanding and love to her. I saw her lips gently curl into a smile, a rare sight.

Jessica, a born-again girl deeply upset by the fundamental volunteers' declaration of the yoga girls' damnation, anxiously broke in. "I don't get it. What you mean, with this Light stuff? Where's Jesus? Why don't we talk about *Him* being *within*? You mean inside me? Like a lightbulb going off somewhere inside me, say wha'?"

Others in our circle rumbled at the sheer silliness of this comment, not meant to be insulting. I was glad those concerned were courageous enough to ask questions.

Everyone was laughing at Jessica's over-the-top lightbulb theory. The mood became less tense. We needed to talk about these hard questions some girls had been holding inside, maybe for their entire lives. The opening-up of these girls' hearts, I figured, would help me to illustrate yoga's spiritual philosophy. It was important for them to know yoga had no religious doctrine. Only descriptions of Oneness. How to attain that state is left to the student. What better tool to convey lofty matters like these than through humor? When our circle quieted again, the discussion went on.

Carrie's mouth was wide-open in shock. She was the new girl that day and she couldn't believe what she was hearing. The contorted face of Amy, who sat next to her on the floor, showed she was troubled as well, having never heard me speak this way before. Neither girl knew what to believe. Some of the girls found it hard to understand that I wasn't a proselytizing pushover like the Christian ladies who told them they were going to hell unless they read the Bible. I laugh easily at jokes, and do the crazy pretzel-poses with them, while reassuring them I was just like they are, when I was younger. Only Katy/Kali and Alex/Durga, my two longest-attending yoga girls, sat contentedly with smiles, having heard me speak like this about the joy of Spirit on other occasions. But I'd never been accused of being a heretic before, which is what the Christians ladies, well-meaning though they may have been, had called me.

"So you saying Jesus has different names?" Kaneesha asked, completely baffled.

"That's right," I cheer. "Jesus is also called many names. Like, the Light of the world, girls," I said. "Also, the Lamb of God, the Prince of Peace, Son of God, and more. He's *Christ Consciousness* and *The Light of God Within,* which many people say is how they think of Jesus. God has many names. In French it's *mon Dieu*, and to Spanish-speaking folks, God is *el Senor*. Allah is the name Muslims use. There's even a stupid joke that dyslexic people pray to their Dog, you know, God spelled backwards."

The circle erupts in squeamish laughter interspersed with shouts of, "You can't say that, Miss!"

I also laugh and say, "Hey, lighten up! We're talking about Spirit here. The Great Mystery. So yes, we can joke about even God.

"What matters isn't the name we have for God, but that we have a *relationship* with God. However that works for us. If the Bible works for you, fine. For me, I started exploring when I was your age. And the person you see before you today is the result of all my research, experiments, and inner and outer exploits.

"It doesn't matter what we call it, as long as we experience *It*, our Spirit-God. Some call God, consciousness. We can call the Inner Light anything—but it really means one and the same Being. Call it Jesus, call it the Chi, Prana, the Holy Spirit, whatever. Spirit is in all creation. So no matter how we refer to this thing that some define with the name, *God*—it's in and of everything.

"The power within each of us is the same many-named power that permeates the entire Universe. People have endless descriptions for the Divine, the sacred in our lives. But there is only one Source, whether you call it Jesus, Great Spirit, or something else. It is your inner source of power, the invisible *'I'* we talk about here, that we become so familiar with in our yoga practice. The source of all in known creation is some form of energy. I prefer to call it consciousness. The Light of Consciousness is another of its common definitions. That's what we mean when we speak of 'the Light within' in yoga," I said, adding, "Namaste."

"So this *is* a religion," Amanda retorted.

"And my mama says I can't mess around with anything that says God ain't Jesus," the blonde waif named Chelsea added.

"No, Chelsea; no, Amanda. Yoga is a philosophy, not a religion. Some people only think of yoga as an effective exercise modality. And that's cool. You can practice whatever religion you want. Some people think the philosophy of yoga helps them become more certain of the spirituality of their faith, and go deeper in their religious beliefs."

"Well, good then." But Amanda still looked doubtful.

Looking around nervously, Chelsea asked, "You sure I won't go to hell? Our pastor said yoga and meditation invited the Devil inside us."

I took a deep breath and tried to steady my now getting-impatient thoughts.

"A lot of people, especially here in the Bible belt, are unfortunately misinformed about everything Eastern. I married my very own born-again, so I know better than most. He's not prejudiced, but the rest of his tribe are highly suspect of me and my love for Eastern mysticism.

"Yoga is an ancient science originally from India. Nothing can harm a person by working with the Light, the consciousness within that yoga reveals to us. There's nothing harmful about pursuing the perfection of your body through yoga, unless you go too far in a pose and don't listen to your *inner teacher* that tells you, shouts in fact! not to push so much. Yes, you could tear a rotator cuff or pull a muscle, a tendon. Sure, you can get hurt. But no, yoga is not a religion.

"So let's be clear: doing yoga does not condemn you to hell. Are we all okay now?

"History tells the story. Our forebears, from earliest cave-dwellers to the extensive Incan empire, focused their religious rituals on the brilliant hovering object so far away, calling it the sun-god, claiming the sun to be the only source of life and light. Sun worshippers were common in ancient times. Humanity has always been searching, celestially and everywhere around them, even in plants, for life's deeper meaning."

"So how does doing a bunch of yoga exercises help us do *that?*" Tiffany asked.

"By first learning to breathe and focus the mind, then attain a pose, we use our bodies and our minds to balance and hold that pose steady. Without a steady, focused mind, the simplest of poses are impossible. Then, after we learn to actually *do* a pose, it makes us feel empowered, and sure enough, we realize that if we can learn to do these challenging poses with our mind-body, then we have a balanced life. The inner teacher that we discover in this manner, which lives within our body, is our connection to God. Our strong, centered mind allows us to go to that place within. Both our everyday lives and our spiritual understanding expand and benefit.

"When our body comes into alignment with our quieted mind, we discover that choices in life await us that are as unlimited as our inner spirit, which is infinite. Einstein said we only use ten percent of our mind's capability. So, you see—when your body and your mind become your teachers, your understanding expands. And God becomes All. I'm just here to turn you on to that. This is yoga. How is this not a beautiful thing?"

The girls went silent at this. The Christian girls looked anything but placated. Some girls looked thrilled, or stared blankly; a few appeared still numb with confusion. I glanced over at Alex. The girl who admitted loving yoga. Her eyes were ablaze as if she'd just discovered the cure for AIDS, cancer, and every other dread disease known to mankind. Durga and Kali appeared to be the only ones who connected to what I was saying. Yet, no one was dissing me anymore. A hush settled over our circle of intention, so I continued.

"It's July, the beginning of hurricane season. We have lots more to discuss than those well-intentioned women scaring you out of your pants. Don't worry, Miss Ursula will be talking to them, telling them to chill with the eternal damnation spiel. Any thing, any place and any situation can be heavenly or hellish, depending on what we make of it.

"When an official hurricane is expected we prepare for the very worst, don't we?"

The girls nodded their heads.

"We may not know about the state of our souls in the afterworld, but we sure know about the dangers of hurricanes here in the present one. Let's stick to what's before us, the present moment, shall we?

"Our lives are like the hurricane season we face," I said to the now-quiet circle. "When we don't prepare for the very worst challenges, we could have a horrendous result. If we prepare we might even enjoy it, as storms are sure powerful manifestations of God's energy. So let's think of doing yoga as preparing for various life-storms, in the same way as we Floridians prepare each hurricane season.

"In yoga we strengthen our inner selves. We batten down the loose parts of ourselves. We repair, heal stuff that's somehow gotten damaged in our life. By doing mind-body exercises we prepare for big upsets that life inevitably brings. Life can knock us down if we're not prepared. If we're not ready to accept the hard as well as the easy. Tough times are, unfortunately, a given for everybody, sooner or later. There's nothing we can do about that. But if we balance our lives by preparing for trouble as well as enjoying the present moment, like we do in our empowering sessions—we're ready for anything."

My eyes met Alex/Durga's. Her luminous face was evidence of how she'd been transformed, from a former depressive who used to cut herself. Her inner brilliance spoke louder than my words. She was living proof that she got this Spirit-thing we've been discussing.

I smiled at her and nodded. I recognized someone whose soul had truly caught fire, purging out the darkness. Just like my teachers showed me to do. Ancient texts describe the *fire of yoga* that is spontaneously ignited within a person. This spiritual fire purifies one's Being, clearing away any obstructions we may have, and brings true contentment.

"Okay, enough talk, girls. Let's end this discussion by saying that the Bible ladies meant well. But they clearly don't know what they're talking about."

I heard gasps from the Christian girls.

"Sorry, but they don't know anything about yoga or the mind-stilling we do here. And when people are without knowledge, they can get scared and attack. But don't worry. Miss Ursula will set these nice ladies straight. They didn't mean to say what they did, and I'm sorry they frightened you. Eastern thought is new to many in America. We can forgive someone who hasn't yet learned how to cultivate a spiritual side as well as the other sides of our humanity.

"So now we'll chant *Om* three times to shift gears from our *normal* to our *spirit*-selves. And then we'll do some kick-butt asanas. Ready?"

CHAPTER 28

it's heee-rreeee

"Yeah, let's kick some yoga butt!" French Fry shouted on the Thursday before Charley. The tough-looking thug girl, so skinny that her Goth bold-font tattoos—running down her un-muscled, stick forearms, spelling out the name of her gang—made her appear decorated by heavy drapes instead of limb-length ink. The others cheered with cries of *Yeah, we're ready!* loudly echoing around the grungy-carpeted common room. The din of laughter sounds animated, fuel for the enthusiastic hatha yoga session that the girls were wild to start. They loved shifting from ordinary to extra-ordinary.

"Man, that floor's too nasty for me!" TraySea/Tara protested as I handed her a facecloth on which she could lay her face for a floor pose.

A lot more than the floor was about to get nasty for the girls.

It's Friday afternoon now, and Alex/Durga is hunkering down with the others, preparing for the eye to strike Bowling Green. She's in the common room with every other soul present at the academy. She's thinking how a balancing pose, like tree, is so good at quieting her mind. "I want to be calm, and not worry. I'm not going to let this hurricane control how happy or fearful I get. I've worked too hard to get this free," Durga will write later in Yoga Thoughts. "And I'm sure not going to give away my peace of mind to the damn weather."

Kali's thinking similarly in her corner of the crowded room. She too, will later write her thoughts in our class journal. "Control, be controlled, or be free, you keep saying, Miss T. Well, ain't no hurricane gonna control me! I guess it boils down to survival of the fittest today. Like every day."

In St. Pete, Ursula is wondering how her girls are faring as she sits feeding her infant, listening to Rafi typing on his keyboard in the next room.

She thinks: "Fear is the biggest storm that affects the human heart. Its attack on our human psyche comes in many sizes, shapes and flavors. From my knowledge, by far the biggest fear the girls at ABG have ever had—is Charley coming right for them."

Ursula listens to the quieting wind outside her window. The brunt of the storm's backside wind-wall has been long gone from St. Pete. The forward wall of the giant system is about to descend on tiny Bowling Green, seventy miles away. Ursula knows these next hours will be the most terror-filled of the girls' lives.

In Lackland, I'm sitting with my husband, listening to the sound of the spiteful wind outside, banging at our safely sheltered home.

I'm remembering all the lead-up to this storm. I too, am thinking about the girls.

"Did I give them enough reminders yesterday?

"Do they have enough tools to endure the onslaught that's coming?"

I assure myself, "Yes. They have everything they need.

"They know, because I showed them myself, that to be in the middle of a storm, of either the natural or man-made variety, is formidable. Fear can overwhelm us, influencing our decisions without our even knowing how. To be even *near* the eye of a hurricane is extremely dangerous. They can't stay in a hurricane's calm eye, but I showed the girls how they can stay within their own smooth spot.

"Yes, the girls will remember that.

"They can choose to reside in their own inner *'I'* pretty much all the time, through awareness of their breath.

"If they can realize just this, they can go through the traumatic experience of a hurricane's eye with ease. If they can trust the inner haven that's always available, they can withstand any chaos outside themselves."

going within ... feeling the connection to my inner power

CHAPTER 29

rebirth – reboot – reform

"What'd you do to change," Kali asked in our circle once, "if you were so much like us, like you say?"

"I got help, that's what. After bottoming out. I joined the spiritual fellowship that teaches how to substitute new, positive actions for my old, destructive addictions. I recommend all of you continue those meetings you've been blessed to have here, when you're on the Outs. And by the way, I'd call prison a low-enough bottom, wouldn't you?

"My spiritual journey began only after putting down the self-sabotaging that surely would have killed me if I hadn't stopped. Only because I was ready then, along came a special teacher I could relate to. And soon, my mind and my heart burst open like a gorgeous exotic orchid that I was then able to discover, right inside me. With practice, I became able to connect to Spirit in all ways. Even recognizing that so-called bad things have their purpose, as change-makers. I'd had that feeling when I was a kid—but like you, maybe, I'd forgotten. It all starts with training those *bad monsters* we talked about, that lived inside me. Those were what kept me wanting to get stoned, be wild, do dangerous things."

I stopped and looked around at the girls who were entranced by my story. I saw they were with me. So I plunged in further.

"Getting clear of negative addictions is what changed my life. I was never the same again. I started learning to love myself."

"How'd you get that feeling?" Sha'ron asked.

"By going within, and feeling my connection to Higher Power, what in AA we call God/Spirit—our HP. No matter what you call it, we must learn how to connect to the 'I' within—our inner power: God within. All these different names just help people connect. In class here, we visit Spirit during our meditation period. Getting quiet helps. For me, so did learning to shut off the voices telling me I was crap, those demons inside, the *monkey-mind* that used to speak so loudly in my head."

"How'd you stop the voices?" Reemie asked.

"By believing that the feeling of incredible joy within me is who *I really am.*"

"How can you trust that the voice inside isn't the Devil?" Royal asked.

"Because to me, God—what those allergic to God call Good-Orderly-Direction—creates all, even what we call bad or evil, like, the Devil."

"How can God create evil?" Sha'Ron was incredulous.

I said, "Think what a boring world it'd be, if Spirit gave us no choices to make! Don't you think the Creator, consciousness Itself, was thoughtful and kind enough to give us conflict, so we could figure things out for ourselves? How boring it would be, just think of it, if everyone were an angel."

"Wait a minute! You think God gave us wars, and people being mean to each other, crank and cocaine, murders, rape, because that's Him being kind to us? You're crazy!" Kali spat out.

I quickly said, "You're putting words in my mouth, now aren't you, Kali? I said that God gave us choices. And Spirit, or God, creates everything. Some call the Source of creation, Sacred or Divine. I call everyday stuff the most sacred of all.

"You can see, girls, this gets pretty complicated, this God/ Spirit stuff. I like to keep it simple. I believe in my Big Heart, that which I experience. Too many people put their slanted, fear-filled thinking over what is good and pure, when we should instead look for ways that all of us are united, not how we're different. When people end up calling good things like yoga—or another person's religion they don't understand—evil, or Devil worship, that's clearly a distortion of Truth. And that's just plain ignorance."

Kali was obviously trying her best to understand.

"Think of it this way," I said, looking right at her. "If you were born a beautiful, filled-with-light baby, which you were, and then, some sixteen years later you decided to kill, maim, plunder, commit crimes and snort crank—and other dumb things you did, except the killing part of course—and maybe even foolishly ran away with your boyfriend on a privileged leave from the academy, which you did … do you think that you deserve to be called *evil* for doing so? Or do you think that you were just confused?"

"I'm not evil," Kali murmured.

"Of course not. You were confused. You were ignorant of the consequences you'd reap from your bad choices like doing drugs and running away. Or maybe you did those things because someone had hurt you once, which was my case, and you wanted to get back at them. You simply didn't know any other way to express yourself except to try to hurt someone, lash out, act out in frustration. But we only hurt ourselves when we think this way. And in your case, Kali, you also hurt your son, because now he doesn't get to see you for an even longer period of time."

Kali remained silent. Her eyes left mine and went to the carpet. She knew this was all true.

"I know you're a good person, Kali," I said. "Now you've been shown another way to live. Miss Ursula has done a great job of rehabilitating all of you. And me, I've tried to teach you about forgiveness, acceptance, detachment; all healing concepts. Our time in class is more than just working on our abs and standing on one leg, right?"

Kali was still quiet. Her body heaved with deep breaths as if relinquishing the habitual defiance that plagued her.

"Kali," I said, "you know there's a part of you that's connected to God, as in your Better-me side. The part of you that wants to love and be loved, and to experience happiness instead of fear and sadness?"

"Of course," she whispered.

"Then wouldn't you say that you have part of God right inside you?"

"I suppose so, if you put it like that," Kali said.

"In yoga we say we create our own hell or our own heaven, right here on earth. The after-life controversy, well, that's another aspect of the Mystery of life. All I know is we can make ourselves so miserable that our lives become hell, or we can choose to embrace the Light of consciousness within, and let the Kundalini energy rise up. By doing this, we allow in the natural bliss of life—and heaven can be ours right now."

I looked around at the totally quiet circle.

"It's up to each of us to choose. If you prefer to think you can't make this hellish place like living in heaven, right now, by changing the way you think; or, if you believe you're going to hell later because you're here in my yoga class, you might want to leave. Because I don't want to be responsible for allowing that kind of thinking."

I wait a few moments. No one budges.

"Okay! So you're all choosing to make your lives happier, more heaven-like. At least to the best of your ability, even in lockup, right here, right!" Everyone laughs and the tension this new concept presented to many of the girls, is broken with relieved giggles and whispered jokes.

"So let's stand, and we'll try some new, fun asanas that some of you have never tried before: the pigeon, the crow, and maybe we'll have time for a baby dragon."

CHAPTER 30

salutations to the
force of nature

E stelle listens to her portable radio she carries now instead of the walkie-talkie, as she sits among the residents and caretakers who are gathered in the common room. Charley's eye is nearing Zolfo Springs. She feels no need to mention this detail to the girls, who have remained perfectly calm from the moment they were brought in single-file and told by the staff to, "make yourselves as comfortable as you can with the pillows and blankets you've brought from your beds."

She hasn't spoken to Ursula on her cell phone for almost two hours.

The eyewall is only 10 miles away but traveling at turtle-speed. Estelle doesn't mention to her girls that Zolfo Springs is where she lives, in the small cinderblock house she bought long ago. She doesn't voice any concerns of her own, keeping to herself any worries she has for the safety of her home and her three children's families. She figures her two daughters, who have babies of their own, are safe in their own homes with their partners. At least they were last time she spoke to them, before she lost phone contact for good. She figures the same is true for her only son, who lives and works in Tampa, which, until last night, had been expecting to get the full force of Charley's landfall, but ended up with only 70 mph winds, a cakewalk.

All three of Estelle's children, she assumes, can take care of themselves, because she's trained them well.

She'd told her daughters long before this day, "These girls here at the academy, now *they* need me. They don't have hardly nobody else that cares for or loves them, 'cept me and Miss Ursula, and the other staff, and Miss T and some others that come and help them."

Estelle knew that if she told the girls in lockup what she really thought about the dangers Charley posed to them, it would distress them needlessly.

She'd told Ursula in a much earlier call, before the lines went dead, "How can it get any worse than it already is? Outside is a nightmare! Thumps and bangs, 'plosives and crashes, and screeches enough for a war zone! I can't let the girls know I be already shaking in my boots. It can't possibly get any worse!"

Just minutes earlier Estelle had announced to everyone, "Girls, it be time to move to the most protected-est part of the facility, the cafeteria. That be the safest area in the building. Has the thickest walls, no outside windows, so Miss Ursula says it sturdiest of all, more than here in the common room. She says we should crowd in there when the eye gets close 'cause the cafeteria has a second floor above it, with offices and stronger beams over us."

For the last hour the girls had been huddling in the common room, quiet and orderly, unusually obedient to whatever the staff told them to do. A rarity at the academy: order and calm. The girls had formed groups and stayed close together in the upholstered chairs and sofas that lined the common room. Quietly they whispered things like, "Hope my mama's okay" and "Wonder if my baby's safe and sound." Concern was on every girl's lips and mind, silent or aloud.

In the corner, the girls' altar was filled to overflowing with bits and pieces of everything the girls could get their hands on. Even a few fingernails bitten off, hair pulled out with or without elastics, or loosened from a hairbrush, bits of paper filled with scribbles. A soda can flipper. An apple core. Lots of good intentions for the girls to look at, to remember, their offerings were like object-prayers. Anything, today, is being used as a request for help, like Miss Ursula taught them to do when they needed extra courage to get through anything heavy-duty scary, like today.

They spent the storm's frontal assault either surrounded by the soft furniture cushions or sprawled on their own bedding around the carpeted floor. They'd been instructed to bring their own bedding "… for your personal comfort." The common room was not dark, because the bulletproof plastic windows let in the afternoon grayness. Now they've moved with their pillows and blankets, single-file from the common room, through the big double doors into the darker cafeteria, where they're told to make a comfortable spot with their bedding on the hard linoleum floor. The electricity has been off for hours. There are no lights other than a couple flashlights and camp lanterns. There's no air circulating in the boarded-up, hot and windowless room.

⚜

The girls are instructed by Estelle and other staff on how things might be in the next short while. The worst part of the storm is nearly upon them.

"Charley's soon comin' down on us," Estelle announces to the assembly as soon as everyone's made their nest on the cafeteria floor. "Radio-man says the eye's for sure gonna hit Bowling Green."

The latest report Estelle hears on her transistor radio puts the eye dead-center in Wauchula, just a few miles south of them. Wind speed is still clocked at 140 mph.

"You doing great, girls," Estelle encourages her wards. "We all going to settle here until this crazy eye passes over. This here be our safe spot. We gonna be just fine, all together."

She smiles, hiding any concerns she may have.

"Remember," she shouts above the increasing din of rising wind and non-stop crashing outside, "what I told you Miss Ursula said to remind you 'bout. That you all brave girls! And can get through anything, just like she says. You girls are the most courageous girls in the whole world right now! Remember that!"

"The eye will feel strange," Mr. Lawrence shouts, for once animated like everyone else. It's unusual for him to talk to the girls except to reprimand them, informing them he's written them up for a critical. His words only reach a few girls who have settled themselves close to where Mr. Lawrence stands.

Estelle walks over and makes a stern face at Lawrence for talking about scary stuff, even though she can barely hear him. She takes back the reins and shouts as loudly as she can:

"We be one-hundred-percent safe here. Look at those thick walls, girls! Miss Ursula guarantees the roof won't be blowing away on us. I feel safer here with you than I be at my own house. And my little place is a fortress, like here be too, believe you me."

Estelle looks around at the girls. They believe her. They've always believed her, because she never gave them any cause not to. She never gave anyone a hard time unless they gave her one first. Unlike Mr. Lawrence, dishing out criticals practically every day, making every girl wonder if she deserved it. By far Lawrence is the least-liked staff, but still, when he sits down, girls crowd around to be near him. He is an adult, after all.

Estelle shouts so everyone can hear her.

"I want you girls to clear the center of the room. Thanks. Now, let's be movin' these steel dining tables from over there to here, in the middle. And stack them to make a big inside-room we can crawl underneath—if necessary. Stack them on top of each other. That be right. You got it, girls. Make it like a big ol' cave in there, so we can crawl in if we haves to. Just in case we need extra protection when the eye gets closer and it be worse than—well, it won't. But Miss Ursula said for us to build this inner room-thingie with the strong cafeteria tables and chairs. So let's do it!"

Eagerly the girls rush to build an interlocking stable structure with the dozen strong steel tables and twenty-something steel chairs. It's finished in minutes. Lawrence, Estelle and the other staff direct the placement of the tables, and shake the final assembly to make sure it's not loose anywhere. Finally, the girls return to their nests all around the perimeter of the central fort, which is just large enough for sixty-two souls to squeeze into in a pinch.

Estelle doesn't speak aloud any of her lingering worries. She knows hurricanes. She knows sometimes it's the sturdiest place that goes first, if the wind catches wrong.

The wind has increased in just these few minutes.

Estelle announces, "Girls, hold onto each other, it make you feel safer. Get ready for the most wild ride of your life!"

CHAPTER 31

suspense

Charley's eye—Estelle's portable radio squawks loudly into her ear—is now less than a mile away. Outside, the wind howls like an army of vengeful witches riding atomic broom-bombs. The girls are senseless with panic, huddled around their tower of stacked-tables in the cafeteria. Everything is a deep gray color except for the meager glow from three battery lanterns Mr. Eric set up for them before he left an hour ago.

He'd been busy since they first got reports that Charley's eye just might head for Bowling Green. He'd secured every window and loose part all around the building, and brought in every item from outside that wasn't nailed down. The facility was as storm-ready as Mr. Eric could make it. Only after making sure of that did he return home, after giving a big hug to each and every one of "his girls." The only man left now was taut-faced Mr. Lawrence, who'd gone quiet again. He seemed distracted holding onto the four or five girls who crept as close as they could to him, putting their heads on his back, his chest, his arms. In spite of himself, he's got these girls helping him hold his tiny transistor radio up to his ear. Looking at this close-knit group of black, white, pink, brown and tan faces, it's hard to discern who's the adult and who's a teenage girl, who's a man and who's a girl.

Kali wrote later in Yoga Thoughts, "I think Mr. L was real nervous 'cause what he kept saying didn't make no sense. Nobody pays no attention to him. Who wants to ruffle his feathers 'cause of all those criticals he dishes out?"

Everyone grows quieter the noisier it becomes outside. Friends and rivals, bullies and bullied, huddle closer. Dislikes, jealousies, hatreds—all melt into irrelevance in this heightened state of alarm. A dozen different groups are now clinging together in the darkened room. Each of the dozen or so groups of three, four, and five girls, sits on blankets on the floor hugging each other, feeling the security of warm comforting bodies. The room—the staff encircling the girls best they can, on the floor themselves, everyone surrounding the towering stack of dining tables and chairs—looks like one living organism with multiple heads and arms sticking out of the soft folds of bedding.

Estelle is hugging two girls tightly to her bosom, two of the youngest inmates who can't stop their hysterics. One cries out repeatedly, "mama!" the other, "my baby!" The other fifty girls are surprisingly calm. Every person there feels as if they're a part of one solid unit of survival. Touching others helps. Fright makes the skin of humans less a separating barrier. We all need comfort, a press of the flesh, a touch, when disturbed. Every five minutes a different staff gets up to walk around the room, mingling, patting, comforting, speaking words of assurance. Even Mr. Lawrence asks when it's his turn, "Y'all right?" to every single girl, excluding none. Everyone is nervous, not knowing what to expect. Bracing for what could come next. Everyone fears what's coming next.

Above the roar Estelle tries shouting louder: "The radio just said the eye be approaching Bowling Green, girls! We be all ready, right? Yes! Now we just relax! And wait. Stay where you seated. Nobody be gettin' up. No more bathroom runs till I says so. We ready to go through what none of us ever been through. We good, we all together. We family here at ABG."

She looks around the room. Nobody can hear her, she realizes. "Girls," she screams anyway, "if you believe in God, now be a good time to ask for help for what we about to go through!"

Only the two girls hugging her hear Estelle. They are praying like crazy, like everyone else in the room.

Outside is such pandemonium that no one inside can hear anything but the storm's shrieks and loud booms going off.

Later on, at our next talking circle, Alex/Durga tells how it was for her, right then.

"I was in a far corner hugging with Shay. Before things got too crazy we looked at each other, and knew we both felt okay. I was in some weird head-space. Felt like I was in the eye of God. I told her that, too. Shay just laughed at me. It felt beyond calm. Like being in love. Not her, Shay I mean. I was observing the storm and wondering about my strange new feeling all at the same time. I was amazed at how happy, relaxed, and safe I felt.

"It was too loud anyway so no one spoke. No one screamed even. All of us were—I don't know—kind of fascinated. Each of us was in our own world. No one knew what this was, or how it would be. I never felt so odd before, ever, but I was okay with that. If I ever felt that way before I don't remember because I was stoned.

"Right there and then, I was thinking, each person must feel everything I do. It was—exciting! We all felt the same exact thing, together. Was it fear? I don't think so. It felt more like—awe. That word sounds stupid, but that's what it was.

"Something so intense happening made me think I had to pee. Excitement rushed everywhere in my body. I could feel my veins. I looked at them, they weren't popping out of my skin. Blood pounding in my forehead's veins, down in my toes. I kept squeezing my insides so I wouldn't be bothered with needing the bathroom. The feeling of suspense was—a high! I felt hypnotized by my own feelings. It was better than the highest high I've ever done—and I was stone-cold sober. My body seemed stronger; my mind was blank, but I was happier than I'd ever been in my life.

"Waiting for it to arrive, then going through it—added something huge to my life. This was the biggest thrill I'd ever known, a hundred times bigger. God is awesome! I've been trying to feel something this intense, inside me, all my life. Maybe, when I grow up, I can become some kind of storm pilot, and drop that stuff Miss Ursula told us about, the silver iodide they release into storm centers. Who knows?"

ShakespearesDelight shares how it was for her in our after-Charley circle:

"For sure, every girl there in the cafeteria was a thrill-junkie, like me. Probably one or two of the staff as well," Shay giggled. "Maybe that's why Mr. Lawrence has always been so hard to read, 'cause deep inside he's more like us than a guard. Chasing extremes, being bad on purpose is what got us girls locked up.

"We all know how alive it made us feel to be doing dangerous stuff. The chemicals, the boys, the robberies. Except for those two crybabies, I bet all the girls were getting off on this scary shit we were going through. That bad-ass hurricane eye about to pounce on us—feeling it got me off. I was higher'n a kite. But I felt calmer than ever before. Both things. Strange, huh?

"Sure, I was terrified of what might happen. But more than that, I was amazed at how in my gut I felt safe. And this storm was just a storm, not my death squad or something. I felt that center of calm you talks about all the time, Miss T, I felt it! I was scared, excited, nervous—yet calm—I was everything! I never knew I could get so high on just my feelings. My feelings amazed me, and—please don't laugh at me, Miss T—I wanted to stay in that place forever, if I could.

"I'm tellin' y'all it was the weirdest thing I've ever felt! Have you ever been so stressed to the point where you're actually calm? Like you accept your fate?" Shay looks around at all the heads nodding in unison.

"Well, that's where I am."

After Shay, Laronda/Leela wants to share:

"That calm place inside me was completely new for me.

"For the first time in my crazy f'd-up life, I felt a natural happy feeling. Like I do when I'm meditating here in class. Boy, did that blow me away. I never knew I could be so scared, but be so peaceful at the same time. It was intense, Miss T! Even more exciting than when I'm on drugs, or having sex, or plotting with my gang for our next car heist.

"I felt so alive! It felt like my life is okay, just the way it is. And I'm not scared to be released no more. I want to be that kind of happy. Now that I know I can, like how the storm showed me I don't need to do a thing to change, to make my feelings more intense, like druggin' or thuggin', I mean. I can just be me. This must be what you been telling us, to be content with just *what is*."

After the next week's class, Durga came up to me to say goodbye, for good. Her release was in just a few days. She wanted privacy to say what she didn't want the other girls to hear.

"Since going through that storm," Alex smiles, her eyes dancing everywhere but with mine, "I'm totally okay with what's happening here, right now. Now I know what it feels like to be in the middle of that inner *'I'* you always talk about. I couldn't wait to tell you, Miss T—how I was in that place you taught us about, the whole time we went through the eye. And you know what?"

"What, Durga?" I ask.

"I wasn't scared at all," she answers, her eyes lifting now, burning brightly, searing right into mine. "I'm ready to be released. I'm ready for whatever comes my way. I feel strong now. That storm made me feel totally cool about everything. This sounds way weird I know—I sat and watched and felt everything around me. I held onto Shay and she to me, but we weren't afraid. Outside the cafeteria, outside the walls, outside and inside me, too, I guess, I realized everything … right at that moment … everything was just how it's supposed to be. And it wasn't upsetting. It was … just happening."

With liquid-black eyes fixed steadily on mine, she said, "It stunned me, Miss, how beautiful that fierce stuff is. It made me cry. It was like knowing God for the first time. Not someone telling me about it. Me knowing, myself."

CHAPTER 32

roar

This is adapted from what Kali told us about her experience,
at that same circle:

Katy/Kali sits tightly holding her best friend Ann Marie, feeling the warmth of another human body, their arms and legs intertwined. Their hips and heads make them appear as Siamese twins. Their bodies snugly fit into a friendship-sized cell. The deafening roar of the eye is upon them.

The terrifying sensation fills Kali's body, her head, with white-black-purple-green-noise discord. She can't think. She can't move. She's frozen. She clings to Ann Marie. Not from fear but in need of comfort, the human touch, the closeness of something familiar, while she's being sucked into the middle of hell-on-earth.

She can't run. She can't move a muscle or blink, or even swallow. Kali doesn't know if she's breathing still, or if she's even alive.

She sits, rooted to the floor, sprawled on top of her familiar blue-and-white-pansies quilt. She has no thoughts. She's merged with the storm, because in all ways, absolutely, she's part of the roar itself now. All around her are bulky shapes, the others. Ann Marie and she are one, in union, with no separation whatsoever. Kali doesn't know if anyone else is alive or dead. Has the roof blown off? Where am I?

Who am I? *What* is this? Kali, in the middle, is filled with ROAR. All noise, wind, married to the tempest that's now part of her.

She has no choice.

She must surrender to the storm, or—

She remembers her hours of practicing: "Breathe ... feel connected to the power within ... I am filled with power ... I am connected to All ... I am ..." she feels the breath of courage filling her with an inner Light ... "part of this invisible power that surrounds us ...."

CHAPTER 33

inner space

Alex speaks to me privately about her hurricane experience:

I sat with Shay. She didn't move at all. Me neither. I felt everything, though.

I couldn't believe how great it felt to be alive! I know what that means now!

All the times I've cut, seeing the blade enter my flesh, I got off on looking at the blood as it bubbled up and started to flow. That was another me. From another life. A long-ago nightmare me.

That storm made me feel I'm here. I'm present. I don't want to check out no more.

I felt everything.

I was there, Miss! In my *'I'* you keep telling us about. I never knew I could trust it, but I do now. I wasn't scared at all.

I never want to leave it, either. Ever again.

All around us was hell and damnation. Like being laid out on train tracks, being run over a thousand times each second. The noise made everything vibrate, the walls, the floor, my blood.

The relief of feeling safe inside was so much greater than that storm's beating.

I felt like, I am part of this! I am real! My realness counts!

From now on, I'm going to stay in this place inside, try to at least, for the rest of my life. Here, I feel good. I know who and what I am. I'm a part of this greatness. Charley and me, we're no different. We're both part of the blinding light coming from God's eye. All of us are; some of us bigger sparks, some smaller, that's all.

CHAPTER 34

the dancing one

A fter the storm passed, I'm sitting quietly on the couch with Will, for some reason I'm thinking of the burning bush story of the Old Testament. I'm thinking how intense it is, being shown the full power of what life around us really is. And how it may be too much for the average Joe and Mary, how sacred life really is. How divine it is, to be alive! Those folks in ancient times we read about in the Bible, all they could accept first-hand of the Spirit-thing was that ordinary bush spontaneously, mysteriously going up in flames instead of the unlimited power of consciousness—like we've just been through, living through a close hit of a killer-hurricane.

And now—the girls over at ABG, are right in the eye. I know they're experiencing this Force to reckon with, or it's just now passed.

I'm overwhelmed, stunned, just imagining what each incarcerated girl must feel. I can't imagine it. I just hope they are safe. I won't know for quite a while, not till tomorrow, how they did. For now, I continue to send my thoughts of comfort and strength to them and their caretakers

At home in St. Pete, Ursula is thinking about the girls' altar she'd created for them in the common room. Then she looks over at the one

in her own sparse but comfy home she shares with Rafi and their son, who's napping now, happily fed, warm and safe.

Ursula reflects on all the symbolic objects she has put on her home altar, and how she encouraged the girls to put tokens on theirs, amulets reminding them to seek more peace, happiness, balance, love, luck—whatever inner stuff they need more of.

Ursula gets up from her chair and walks over to the chest-level shelf in the kitchen that doubles as her altar. She feels the need to give it another offering. She heads outside, smells the strong ozone in the highly charged air, and plucks a fresh sprig of plumbago, miraculously only slightly battered from the recently passed storm. A bush of the violet clusters of starry flowers grows prolifically in her yard. She returns to the altar and places the lone pale bloom she found on the shelf alongside the shells, pebbles, and a tiny stone Buddha already there.

Now Ursula feels she's present, at the academy, with her girls.

"I'm with them now, that's what this flower means to me," she says softly.

Closing her eyes, Ursula wants to feel what they are going through. She feels connected, just by willing herself to be with them. She sends her love and abundant courage to every person, the girls, the staff, all who are gathered in the darkened cafeteria, where she'd told Estelle to take them, long before they knew the eye would strike so close.

She recalls how she'd taught the girls to use their altar. How she'd bought a bouquet with her own funds, and given each girl a flower. "Put it on the shelf and wish for something, anything! And when you see your flower during the day, you'll remember what your heart desires."

Ever since that time, the girls' altar had always been filled with unusual gifts, and periodically Ursula had to clear the old away, always at a House Meeting, to start anew.

Ursula remembered the time MaryAnn brought up how she hated teZa at one House Meeting. She'd told the disturbed girl who'd had a less-than-enjoyable experience in yoga class, "Get that anger out of your heart, MaryAnn. If you don't like Miss T, now's the time to say so."

Then so many other girls spoke of their admiration for the yoga teacher that by the end of the session, the Miss T-basher swore, "I'll try to stop hating her so much."

"Let's put something up on the altar right now," Ursula told MaryAnn and the others, "to remind the entire school of what Miss teZa does for all of us."

Molly/Matrika brought an orange she'd stuffed in her pocket after lunch. Rene/Viveka gave a wilted pink carnation she'd been given by a volunteer at hobby time. Sha'Ria/Maya brought to the shelf a piece of shredded napkin from lunch. Alex/Durga found a button on the floor to offer. Shay had a wrapper from yesterday's snack in her pants pocket. Then, after the meeting, all day long girls brought odds and ends until the shelf in the corner of the common room was overflowing with tokens, representing respect and love for their yoga teacher.

At the end of that House Meeting, everyone, even the girl who swore Miss T was a phony, was buzzing with how much they appreciated her. The power of the group, and the action of placing dedicated trinkets—a loose clip, a bit of fuzz, a strand of hair—portrayed how strongly the girls felt about someone another had disparaged unfairly.

"This is how group conscience works," Ursula reminds herself now, staring at her plumbago bloom, remembering the many times she has described the powerful tool of intention to her girls.

Ursula muses on what the lavender blossom she's just placed on the shelf represents.

Empowerment is what I offer the hunkered-down girls at the academy, she thinks as she gazes at the blue flower on the ledge. I hope they remember how comforting it is to stay in the peaceful inner calm—their magical inner 'I' as teZ calls it—during whatever storms they're going through.

Yes, she continues, there will always be storms in life and in Nature. And there's always the safety spot inside us to stay in, if we want.

Ursula checks on Vrish. Her perfect, peaceful sleeping baby. Looking at him, she remembers how it was after 9/11. Not just in New York City, but everywhere she went. People felt more connected to others than they had for ages. Disasters have a way of doing that.

She bends over to caress Vrish's cheek. One thing I know from that awful day—she nods in assurance—when tested in crises of any kind, humanity comes together.

Ravenously, the eye consumes everything it can, swallowing whole or partly, large and small, anything, everything.

Countless tiny tornados spin off madly from the outer rim of the eye, offshoots of Charley's funneling, voracious vortex.

A house and a business right next to the academy are swept away. Halves and whole, limbs and trunks and entire colossal trees are thrown everywhere by greedy winds, tossed like bowling pins. A century-old oak is uprooted and lands on someone's house behind the academy, the residents thankfully evacuated. A sink-hole opens up alongside the main highway running through Bowling Green, shockingly sucking in half a house and the front of two cars, and part of the parking lot of a nearby warehouse.

The only witnesses to Charley's insane all-consuming commotion are its own deadly winds, continuous sparks of lightning bolts, and solid sheets of sidewise-rain. Everything else hides.

Estelle sits in the cafeteria, girls huddled tightly all around her. Estelle sees her inner-Self so clearly. She's a strong black woman, a free and easy Light Dancer. Her spirit is as powerful as the wind itself, safe from the fierce beast outside the academy's doors.

She's not one of the women she hears about, who run with the wolves ... she *is* the wolf.

The eye has passed. Charley's back wall slowly lowers its wind walloping velocity.

There's a crispness in the air, a release from the earlier tension felt everywhere, Estelle realizes. She shouts, "We be safe!" The reality that they have survived begins to still the rhythm of her fast-beating heart. Earth now starts to breathe more normally because the tempest has moved on.

"Girls, it be over!" Estelle cries out when the wind dies down so she can be heard.

Estelle's breath and heartbeat match the storm's dissipating wind. She's had her calm, now she's coming back to ... what? Responsibilities. Her girls. Her family.

As she helps girls gather their things Estelle can't help thinking how the awfulness of the past hours seems like a mirror of the ebb and flow, the good and bad of all in the heavenly creation she loves studying about in the Bible. "Charley be like the world gone crazy. That eye be like earth's having bad breath," Estelle laughs despite herself. "Not like my sweet life. Sure is a crazy carnival ride we be havin' here on this rotating planet we live on. What's next? Bring it on! Lord Almighty, I be ready!"

The Dancing One breathes. Mother Nature's energy makes our planet and all upon it laugh and live, all in harmony.

Estelle knows there's only so much these girls' roughed-up souls can soak up in the short time she has with them before they're on the Outs.

As she gathers herself, she feels the girls around her awaken and emerge from their internal solace, deep inside themselves, where they sought shelter during the storm. Estelle wants to shout and tell them about love, about trust, about keeping joy alive in their hearts. No matter what shit-storm happens to or around them.

But instead, she slowly stands and stretches, and says, "It's time, girls. Time to gather your things and head back to your rooms. Single-file. Quietly, please."

CHAPTER 35

huh?

If Hurricane Charley could speak, what would It have to say?
Why does It torment us so? I've asked the big bad storm these
questions, taking liberties as every writer does.
This is what the storm tells me:

Freedom is Being.
Control has nothing to do with Being, except in the minds of people who define big ideas by small incongruous things called words. Control is just a word. It can change or disappear, as it has and will, with every new generation, every new political battle, every new uprising of culture.

Freedom for humans is being in tune with the ways of Nature, like we storms are.

I can only control myself, me, hurricane Charley. Beings who get in my way think I control them, but … they are the ones who chose to get in my way. I'm just being me, a force of Nature. I'm not trying to dictate to them. Get it? I'm just being me, a big bad storm.

Every person, whether in jail or at home, in a refugee camp, a presidential limo or a homeless shelter, has to figure this out for themselves.

Freedom is a state of mind. It has nothing to do with one's surroundings or situation. Being is Freedom. Freedom is Being.

For anyone who doesn't grasp this, who still thinks freedom is about who they control or don't control, who they do or don't have on their side, I—big bad Charley—am here to say:

The biggest challenge of life is to let go of controlling or being controlled by others, and to get real. We are meant to live in tune with our commonality. Every human is a supernatural being, if they're awake enough to realize this. Even if you're in prison, or stuck in your own prison of perception, your jailers have no control over the free soul you really are.

We storm systems, and you blood-and-guts children of the One, the shared Source—Mother Nature and Her phalanx of Names—each must answer for our self: Are we free?

CHAPTER 36

stillness

For days afterwards the academy will be out of power. It takes many tries before Mr. Eric finally gets the faulty generator running, so until then, the girls have no running water, air-conditioning, lights, or anything else requiring electricity. In the weeks to come Mr. Eric will have to wear a wrist brace because of the bruising he suffered from a door that blew loose during the storm's approach. Just before the eye hit, a side kitchen door came unbolted, so while Mr. Lawrence held it, Mr. Eric nailed it shut, and then braved the wind to get home, a few blocks away. Eric's house is made of cement cinder blocks, so he knew it was as safe as the strong facility the girls were housed in.

The front end of Charley was still pounding Fort Meade, a few miles north, as its phenomenally calm eye passed over Bowling Green. Going through the eye of a hurricane is like being in a giant reverse-blade blender set at full speed, with only a short respite between two opposing forces, when the cosmic switch is thrown that controls directions.

By 8 p.m. that Friday the 13th, the girls began to unwind their interlocked limbs from one another. The worst was over. Miss Estelle has just told them they can go back and sleep in their own beds now.

Everyone is exhausted. Now they can stop pressing their white knuckles together, biting sore lips, sucking on nails nibbled bloody.

The entire three hours of the eye's journey over them was more exhilaration than frightening. This was the Mount Olympus of highs for caught-for-now druggies. Only this high was free, much more potent, longer-lasting, and a way more intense hammering than anything any girl had ever experienced.

For now … the state of emergency … was over.

Every single person there, inmate or guard, was glad to be alive.

Soon Mr. Eric let himself back in by removing the nails he'd used to bolt down the outside door. He and his wife Gladys had a similar experience to what those at the academy lived through. For those whose homes are sturdily built structures, life in the hurricane and cyclone zones is much less stressful. Mr. Eric brought a case of bottled water with him from his home. Estelle was relieved to see him. And the water. She was concerned that if something had happened to their faithful custodian, who'd nailed all the outside doors shut before he went home, they'd be in trouble if they required outside aid. Her cell phone was worthless. But Mr. Eric, as always, showed up just in time.

For now, everyone is happy to still be breathing. The darkness doesn't scare them, but the heat is suffocating. They have only snacks to eat until Mr. Eric can bring out the supplies he'd packed for them. A late dinner will be boiled rice and beans on a camp stove.

Some odd leftovers remain in the cafeteria that were brought in before they'd barricaded the building: a box of candy bars, some apples, a couple bags of chips, but only a few bottles of water.

On this airless, hot and humid night, with the facilities' shatterproof windows hermetically sealed, the girls file back to their rooms, dragging their damp bedding with them. Although hot and sweaty, everyone will sleep soundly tonight. More exhausted than they've ever been in their lives.

CHAPTER 37

breakthrough—
from scared to sacred

Whether a storm originates from Nature or is born of our own anguish, both disturbances are real to those who experience them. Emotional inner storms have their calm center within, where a person can find peace even in the most crippling pain. Just as a hurricane has its eerie eye, an individual's life-storm has its own inner *'I'* in which we can take shelter anytime, anywhere.

The trick, of course, is finding how to safely get to that inner sanctum. Staying in the core, the *'I'* within, through all of life's ups and downs, is the ultimate challenge of one's spiritual journey. Finding how to do this makes being alive a game of remembrance, because we came from the same universal Source, Oneness, when we first arrived on this planet at birth. As a child, if we aren't properly nurtured, and learn how to maintain this inner connection, to trust the *'I'*—life itself becomes a paradoxical game of hide-and-seek. Trying to hide or heal from pain, sorrow, and constant disappointments.

We're all born with childlike innocence, with core centers of utter peacefulness. We forget that part of us, our true nature, remains forever connected to the eternal truth of our energetic makeup. Without nurturing, the Divine aspect of our nature becomes obscured, and sadly, some of us never re-discover or return to *It*.

Life is filled with some horrendous life-storms. Entire nations feel sadness and shame over wars, and all of us cringe over injustices of humankind's corruption. Society is toxic with human conflicts and environmental atrocities. My own life, as everyone's, has been filled with mini-trauma. Yet today I choose to remain in the inner state despite the outer conflicts that certainly surround me. I choose to stay connected to Love, which is The Eternal, instead of allowing outside circumstances rob me of my hard-won serenity. From this center, I operate most effectively as a spiritual activist, my small contribution to make our world a better place.

Besides, it's a lot more fun when I'm feeling this way. This is the choice we all make. I must never forget that my inner *'I'* is Self-love.

Tupac the hero, is now usurped in the girls' eyes by Mr. Eric, the lanky Jamaican who can fix anything, who finally gets the A/C running after days of agitating heat and humidity. Those bulletproof windows—which don't open—are bad news with no air conditioning. The high anxiety of going through the eye is only the beginning of the girls' lives being tested, as all of us are as well. It falls to Ursula and the other instructors to help the girls integrate the impact of having met this ordeal head-on. Having gone through any cataclysmic event, in the calm of acceptance, is how they can stay in the *chill* of the inner *'I'* anytime they wish.

"All you have to do," Ursula instructs them at the next House Meeting, "is remember: You can choose to be calm. If you forget to go within, you'll be swept away by your emotions just like those trees got uprooted by Charley's crazy wind."

It was a full year earlier when another storm like Charley hit, in the full moon's energy warp. It was the kind of day and night when Ursula expected chaos. She had extra staff on duty, as many as were on hand for other storms. A few of the girls who would go through Charley were there. Katy/Kali the absconder, who'd recently had six months added on to her sentence after her foolish drug-and-sex binge. Alex/Durga was there too, the former-cutter who'd be released days after Charley gave her such a profound life lesson.

August 11, 2003 was a hot and sticky, muggy afternoon. The girls at ABG were pissed-off more than usual because they weren't free, there wasn't enough food, neither phone calls nor deodorant. Everyone was crawling out of their stinky skins. You name it, they were angry about it, big time. But there was another reason besides the weather and the phase of the moon, as Ursula told me later, that the girls went berserk that Monday.

This was the first time my family and I had gone on a vacation since I'd begun teaching at the academy the year before. As Ursula explained to me afterwards, "They were even more restless than a usual full-moon agitation because your presence had become important to them. Your coming each week maintained a sense of peace in the entire population, ever since you first showed up to teach them. When you went on vacation, the girls' usual reminders of how to be calm were suddenly gone. I'm afraid those two weeks of no yoga sessions took their toll on the academy's psyche. Your usual yoga girls did their best, but—".

Miss Estelle told me when I saw her upon returning from my vacation, "You be proud of the you-ga girls, Miss teZa. They the only ones who stayed in control of themselves." She still struggled with the name of my class.

After two weeks of the population not receiving yoga's *communal benefits*, as Ursula called it, the girls fell all too easily back into their old habits of uncontrolled hysteria. The shocking event that happened could also be attributed to the moon's effect, according to Ursula.

"It's well known in my field of mental health that the full moon adversely affects people, as well as tides of the ocean," she'd told me well before this particular full moon. She also mentioned, on many occasions, "Your coming here was felt as a positive influence, from the moment you first came to give us that demonstration class."

When I arrived that day, a year before Charley, Ursula told me. "Your absence was evident in the general mood at the academy. I've not seen everyone so disturbed in the entire year you've been coming. It was like a bomb had gone off in there."

The trouble started at lunch. Seventeen criticals and four takedowns—an all-time record—before lunch even began.

"Then—pure mayhem," Ursula said, "as soon as the trays were served."

Food was thrown. Screams, plates flying, milk and juice sprayed everywhere. Punches. Bites. Kicks. Hair-pulling.

Anarchy reigned. No one obeyed, not even when multiple takedowns were going on simultaneously. The staff had to stop to defend themselves. The violence was out of hand. This was a full-blown RIOT!

Cops were called and arrived within minutes.

The girls who didn't settle down right away were arrested (that's right! Arrested while in lockup) and seven key troublemakers were hauled off to jail.

When I arrived that Thursday immediately afterwards, Ursula greeted me with the urgent news. "I'm convinced your efforts saved us from a worse disaster than it was. Way more girls would have been taken away to real jail if it wasn't for your yoga girls."

I was stunned silent.

"Katy and Alex, Alice, Shay and Sha'Ria were the first ones who got out of the fracas and huddled in a corner. They stayed there and observed the others going bonkers. We're lucky there was only one broken bone from all that violence. Pretty soon there was a group of girls, all your students, sitting together, refusing to participate, staying as calm as they could while everybody else was throwing punches and anything that wasn't tied down."

I said, "God, I'm shocked. But it's heartening what you're saying, Ursula, about the yoga girls."

"I'll say. The only ones who chose not to participate in the riot were your students. The rest got real ugly and real vicious. Thrown chairs bloodied quite a few noses, besides the one broken arm. Luckily we had no other serious injuries except cut fists and heavy bruising from the kicking, and chairs and trays whizzing everywhere. I ducked under a table until the police arrived. Thankfully a cruiser was nearby in Bowling Green."

"I'm blown away, Ursula," I said, aware of a tightness in my chest, thinking of these girls who milled around us as we two women spoke—teenagers with such ordinary faces, like-me-or-leave-me-alone smiles or smirks, sets of both fear-filled and hopeful eyes—in such a preposterous state of useless, dramatic upheaval. Berserk is the only word for the bizarre scene Ursula was describing. Absurd that the girls could turn lunch into a senseless food-fight of such magnitude, a fist-and-foot war.

Ursula smiled and patted my shoulder. "You'd be proud. To me, this is a powerful testament to the tangible and substantial effects of the practices you've brought here. Left to their own devices, much of humanity still clings to their lower tendencies. Mindfulness brings monumental change to not only individuals, but—like it has here, and instantaneously—to a community comprised of both those who participate in mind-body work, and those who don't."

Estelle greeted me that day after the riot with a big bear hug, and more news about what happened.

"Miss, those you-ga girls did everything they could to stop the fight, but they failed. So they just sat down and watched from a corner, as every other girl went crazy."

Mr. Lawrence barely glanced at me, acting as if I were a complete stranger, when I arrived that Thursday and discovered what had happened during my brief absence. When he passed me to take his seat in the back of our yoga class, as usual, I nodded his way, and he nodded back.

all of us are holding the inner Light so strongly!

CHAPTER 38

transformation

After Charley, it became obvious, little by little, as the days ahead revealed, how facing a wall of fear affects a person—some more drastically than others.

Call it a miracle, but Estelle was the first to notice.

When she finally gets through to her boss sometime the next morning after the storm, the head staff has much to report. Right after saying how calm and obedient the residents had been, she had excitedly added: "Miss Ursula, so strange! I noticed Lawrence watching over the girls like his little sisters instead of his usual delinquents. He be different, like, *pleasant*, ever since this hard time passed over us."

Ursula is pleased to hear this. She didn't look forward to having to let Lawrence go, but his attitude had become so negative lately, that before the storm she'd actually been considering firing him, as short-handed as the ABG staff was.

As the days progressed after Charley, everyone witnessed the change for themselves.

"The storm must have shown him how their spirits, their insides be beautiful, like you and me knows already," Estelle whispers to Ursula a few days later, nodding in Lawrence's direction.

Both women smile. They notice the shift in Lawrence's attitude, evident in both small and large ways. Most obvious is the abrupt stop of his criticals, which he used to lavishly dish out for the smallest of infractions.

"From wise-ass to wise uncle, that be Lawrence these days," Estelle jokes to another staff a few days after Charley, even though she'd never said anything before about his prickly personality. She never judges. Estelle always accepts people as they are. But when someone decides to make something better of themselves, she makes a point to notice and compliment them on their effort. She rewarded such personal efforts in her own three children, all her girls at the academy, and now with her fellow staff.

"Mr. Lawrence," she said, walking straight up to him one day not long after Charley. "I gots to admire you. You doing a fine job at being a better person lately, and I wants to congratulate you for that."

Estelle welcomes any cause to celebrate self-improvement in anyone. She also likes to make people feel good about themselves.

"Your heart gone from nut-hard to sweet-soft, mister, and I here to tell you it pleases me no end, Lawrence. Un-huh."

His face beamed like the sun peeking out from behind a cloud after a mean downpour. Mr. Lawrence put down his walkie-talkie on the arm of a nearby sofa, and to the astonishment of the three other staff who witnessed this first-ever event in the common room that day, he hugged his compassionate supervisor, old enough to be the loving mother he never had.

CHAPTER 39

freed from the prison of false perception

Throughout the duration of Charley's direct hit, Ursula figured towers were toppled and it'd be a while before cell reception got restored. She stayed connected to Estelle and the girls, though, using her own methods. When she saw on the weather channel that the storm had passed Bowling Green, finally, at 9 p.m. she called the police in Wauchula. She was assured someone would stop by to check on the academy. All Ursula could do was pray, which she did non-stop, when she wasn't tending to Vrish or hanging with Rafi. A polite officer called her back around ten to assure her everything was all right at ABG, except they had no power. She wouldn't know any more until she arrived by car early Saturday afternoon.

The usual two-hour one-way commute took her and her three co-workers almost five hours, there were so many obstructions on the road. But they finally made it.

Ursula discovered that ABG was hanging on, barely. The toilets wouldn't flush, and it was hotter than Hades with no A/C and no interior breeze, although Mr. Eric would remove crucial panes of plastic soon after she arrived, upon her direction. There wouldn't be any running water for the next three days. Mr. Eric was frustrated in his repeated efforts to repair the generator that kept failing to start.

Food for the girls was carried in by whichever staff was on duty. The usual caterers, also without water or electricity in their own kitchen, were unable to fulfill their contractual obligations. Yet somehow three squares a day appeared. One of the staff drove miles away to the nearest grocery store or fast-food joint for each meal.

Gratefully the facility remained intact, as did Mr. Eric's sturdy concrete cottage, while all around them the village of Bowling Green was laid waste. Every building had its roof or exterior partially or entirely blown away. The little village was heart-wrenchingly torn up.

Within hours after Charley's eye smashed through Bowling Green, a caravan of the National Guard, men and women, arrived with food, water, and surplus generators, none of which, unfortunately, were powerful enough to run ABG's air conditioner. The Guard appeared before dawn on Saturday. Estelle, unable to reach Ursula or Wayne to get either of their formal permission, agreed without hesitation to let them set up their regional headquarters in the common room at the academy.

"It be best place for them to set up," Estelle told Ursula when she showed up. "I not sayin' no to them big shots in uniforms." She complied with the Guards' urgent request when they pulled up as the first streaks of a clear new day's sun cracked the horizon. "Your place is the biggest, most centrally located in this entire hard-hit area," the commander informed her. Ursula concurred when she later reached ABG.

The girls were excited to see the agencies respond so quickly to emergencies, observing how people come together to help. "Just like we done during the terrible times after the terrorist attack in 2001," Estelle said to her wide-eyed charges. "We humans do real good in any emergency. All the TV-people say we do better in tough times."

Not a one of the girls or Estelle's staff was a history buff, so seeing an up-close rescue operation was an eye opener for everyone.

From breathtaking beauty to devilish storms, Nature is always in control of the puny residents of earth. I wanted to make sure I could clearly present to the girls, when I next saw them, what they had just gone through—as an allegory, useful for illustrating a much bigger idea than a mere passing storm.

At home in Lackland, I'm envisioning how to do this. How to discuss with my girls at our next talking circle, the great lesson learned from going through Charley's eye. How being scared can lead some of us to becoming aware of the magic of life. How being frightened to death can turn out to be a good thing, once we come out unscathed, that is.

I remind myself to talk to my girls about how all of life reflects what they've just been through with this emergency: choosing to survive hard times, choosing to take as much goodness out of whatever hand we've been dealt. Accepting the cards we've been dealt with joy, not sorrow. Playing the game of life—and having fun while doing it.

Choosing love, not fear.

Charley taught them how important it is to remain in our inner 'I'—the peaceful, joyous part of us—that's connected to everything. The part that no one but us controls. Because the 'I' is part of Nature, and it's part of our basic nature, too—bad things can't touch us when we embrace our inner Self.

I chuckle, thinking how the 'I' appears, symbolically. The capital letter "I" is grounded to both the lower and the higher planes. I then thought that when the 'I' of each person is cultivated, we experience a more expansive perception of ordinary life. The more a person resides in meditation or contemplation, for instance, the more grounded they are, and at the same time they also pull aside the so-called *veiled portal* that opens up our inner wisdom.

The inner 'I' is the door through which we bust out of the prison of our limited perception.

I wanted to share with the girls how a meditator, with regular practice, becomes able to "see" or "sense" the bigger picture of what mystics define by the aphorism:

There's more to life than meets the eye.

I also need to remind my girls that everything is perfect just the way it is. *They* are perfect just the way they are. I am, and you are too, dear friend. Everything happens for a reason. Even so-called catastrophes have purpose. Just wait and watch. The worst event, in time, makes sense when viewed in perspective, in light of the larger picture. And I'm talking about what happens to our own lives as well as what's happening in world events. Everything happens for a reason. We just don't know what that is until time passes.

In my musings I'm sharing these truths with my students. Them, and not my stepdaughter, Kara, who's the same age as most of my yoga girls. Because I can't share such concepts with Kara, since she refuses to even listen to me, my heart swells in gratitude for my yoga girls, who are so open, so interested, and so thirsty for what I can offer them. Kara wouldn't believe me if I shared these ideas with her. I've tried, believe me. She just rolls her irreverent, dismissive eyes.

For sure, Kara is my most aching life-storm to date. Yes, I miss her loving me. God, how I miss her once blind trust! But I focus on my girls over at ABG instead. And believe that one day I'll discover a greater reason for having lost Kara.

"There's more to this than meets the eye," I remind myself.

What's gone amiss between Kara and me, I haven't a clue. All I know is that, in time, my inner 'I' will reveal that, as well.

Being connected to everything is what the 'I' or God-within means to me. That's what I want to remember to express to my girls. It's what I also long to share with Kara. But ... I will have to wait till she learns to love herself first. Then maybe she'll recognize who I am to her.

Later, Ursula will remark to me, "The ABG girls' earlier lives, with so much trauma and drama, empowered them to get through this ordeal of Charley. Emergencies, crises, catastrophes—they help us grow. Pain," Ursula the psychologist assures me, "is like manure for the spiritual garden we grow within. Pain hurts us but it also helps heal us. It's like the ultimate paradox. And once we start getting healed and whole, we begin to experience the ultimate realization— that we are all the same Self, the term Freud and Jung helped coin. I think you call it both the inner *'I'* and ... the One."

When we have our next private talk, Ursula shares other truths that ring out loud and clear to me.

"Our mainstream culture," she says with the authority of a professional health counselor, "honors only the deities of denial. Sadly, disrespect and greed are more popular today than kindness and compassion. Distracted, computerized modern life promotes the opposite of the sacred. Look at the way the kids dance now, like they're fucking—everyone all together, boys, girls, in-betweens—the louder and more deafening to the finer senses, the better.

"In these kids' lives here at ABG," Ursula points out, "and even more when they're on the Outs, it's impossible for them to be quiet, much less have an introspective side. Kids feel life's a race of trying to satisfy their material wants and desires. Finding inner peace within each of us, that's our only hope. You and I know, teZ, that's the only true satisfaction, the only lasting peace we humans can ever count on. Trust our *'I'* as you call it in class, and a person discovers their direct link to the Source of everything. In this world of shifting sand and elusive good will, we're surrounded by ever-increasing, scary, fear-fueled tribes. Hardly anyone remembers that inner joy is the greatest treasure of all."

These moments Ursula and I share make both of us happy, a reminder of our like-mindedness each time we run into each other at the academy, and on the Outs.

"Inner strength," my wise friend says, "how to seek it, how to nourish it—is what you've shown your girls, my dear. You should take heart in knowing that at least a few of them will leave this place carrying that with them.

"The girls who arrive at ABG haven't come here because they've realized they have all the power they need for a happy, rich life, right inside their souls.

"Life has dealt them a serious blow. These girls—no matter what crimes or circumstances brought them to lockup—got blown over by their own stormy lives."

Saturday, the day after Charley hit—Ursula allows the girls from the academy out with their caregivers, to walk around what's left of Bowling Green. She wants them to see for themselves the mind-numbing damage of Nature's full-on intensity.

In this rare instance of not being handcuffed or shackled, *de rigueur* for all off-facility outings, the girls witness for themselves the disaster they survived. They crawl over cliffs of felled trees, side-step dead power and phone lines that lie everywhere. They walk the debris-strewn streets surrounding their undamaged facility. All around their exercise yard, out through the triple-locked-gates entrance, they move in shocked silence. They see mounds of leaf-trash piled high, heaped against the razor-topped fence, its black privacy sheets in tatters, camouflaging the several well-built adjacent new schoolrooms they sit in each day, which sustained minimal damage. Piled up in brown-green drifts, the thick smell of already composting leaves is an outward sign of Charley having wrestled with, but failed to take down, super-strong ABG, their prison-home.

Everywhere the shaken girls wander as they are led by staff through the deserted town, they see total destruction. Senseless shambles. To them it's equivalent to the nightmare they've heard a nuclear bomb attack would be. Around ABG, people's homes and businesses are gone or flattened. Everything they've been seeing outside their plastic security windows—for the entirety of their many months-, often years-long sentences—has been destroyed. Roofs are blown away or collapsed. Homes and businesses, crushed by monster limbs and trunks. A whole line of tall oaks on the one main drag, lie toppled like slammed-down dominoes. Endless miles of electrical poles, knocked-over in tied-tandem as far as the eye can see, resemble kiddie-toys toppled as easily as a game of pick-up sticks.

The girls shudder when seeing for themselves the horror that has wasted this nowhere town they've been imprisoned in. Everywhere they look are the strewn polka-dots of people's lost belongings, resembling raw eggs with sad, broken shells, shards of memories lost forever. The girls acknowledge the truth before them: the ravaging monster of Charley gobbled up all of Bowling Green—except them.

The girls remain silent. Sadness and shock weigh them down as they creep and crawl through the rubble. There's no clear areas for them to walk upright for more than a few steps. Sidewalks and streets are jumbled heaps of shredded vegetation and busted-apart furniture, clothing, and pieces of metal and plastic. At the wretched sight of the devastated mobile park across the street, each girl draws in her breath sharply, grateful to be alive. Some girls are weeping silently.

No burning bush here. This is the raw, unadulterated truth of the unlimited power of God and Nature. The girls accept it without comment. Without a sliver of disrespect.

After Charley hit the academy, some of the girls at Bowling Green were practically catatonic from what they'd endured. High anxiety took its toll on everyone. Week after week for what seemed forever, but was actually only a couple of months of the remaining hurricane season, everyone in Florida would continue to feel powerless—except those who sought shelter in their inner state. There comes a point when human existence is touched so fiercely by unforeseen occurrences, that you have to let go of any expectation of certainty—especially from the weather.

Like one of my yoga girls said in our circle right after Charley, when we discussed those points I'd wanted to present about facing life's inevitable challenges:

"I get it, Miss T! I can either see a rope in the grass as a snake, or what it really is—just a rope. I'm not gonna let life get me down no more," Eva/*Chid* (*the Inner Light*) said, to everyone's vigorous nods of agreement.

The new girl, Cheyenne, laughed. "Yeah, I'm with Chid! I choose to not be afraid of anything anymore, like her. I want my life, even while here at the academy, to be the heaven I make of it."

postscript

Instead of putting up and taking down our boarded-up windows during the dizzying 2004 hurricane season, most people in our region left everything—supplies, taped-up glass, readied flashlights and torches—exactly as it was until the end of November. By then, we'd endured seven major hurricane strikes.

Three weeks after what began with Alex, followed by barely-there Bonnie, then that nasty mammoth Charley, we endured another storm alert for what seemed our state's never-ending nightmare. Next came fierce Frances, and invincible Ivan, and—dare I say it—jubilant jive-ass Jeanne, the last storm that hit us not just once, but after it did its schizophrenic 360-degree out in the Atlantic, Jeanne came back across Florida to kick us a second time, only to peter out in the Gulf of Mexico.

Before reaching the US mainland, Jeanne had killed thousands. It targeted poor, bad-luck Haiti on Hispaniola, the large island shared with the Dominican Republic, where an earlier killer-storm, one I'd lived through back in the 70s, also took thousands of souls.

Our family became so accustomed to caving-up, playing board games, huddling and praying together, that storm jokes were no longer amusing. Florida managed to miss the more severe damage inflicted on the unprotected island-countries of Grenada, the Bahamas, Jamaica, and Haiti, all of which took the full brunt of the killer-storms in that off-the-wall season of 2004.

And the world knows how Hurricane Katrina would decimate New Orleans the following August, in 2005.

For weeks afterwards, convoys of bright-colored electric-company trucks came from Georgia and as far away as Tennessee, the Carolinas, even Arkansas, to help rebuild the damage the rudest storms, Charley and Francis, did to our region. Every inch of the interconnecting power grid had been bludgeoned to death. Infrastructure recovery took months. For those whose lives were personally damaged, the repair took years. When the cyclonic winds of Frances hit Florida, its wake was as wide as the state of Texas.

The storm gods dance their hurricane and tsunami insane jigs over the endless expanse of our watery world, pushing the hapless land and its inhabitants out of their way. What the water-world doesn't test of our strength and long-lasting endurance, earthquakes, landslides and wild fires do.

After Bowling Green was flattened, a much-diminished Charley churned toward Winter Haven. Then it edged close to the outskirts of the metropolis of Orlando, its gusts slowing to a mere 110 mph before exiting Florida just north of Daytona. The storm's hours-long joyride through our state caused more than thirteen billion dollars of damage.

More than a decade after Charley, ABG is no longer.

"The juvie correctional system has gone backwards," Ursula told me recently. "All the things I worked so hard for in rehabilitating the girls, integrating schoolwork with empowering modalities like yoga and meditation, have been eliminated because of budget cuts and lack of support. Now the entire prison system for juvies is structured for boys. Girls' facilities are only *painted pink*, as we say in the field, but none cater to a girl's special needs.

"The prison system is going back to using punitive discipline instead of inspiring real long-lasting change and healing," Ursula sadly stated.

We're both crushed and disappointed about this.

Ursula had prayed me up. She battled to keep empowerment/stress reduction sessions alive as juvie rehabilitation tools. After losing ABG's Medicaid funding, she became frustrated and went into private practice. Ursula advocates for compassion as love with action. She taught her girls, and her own kids (she later gave birth to a second son), to be accepting and not judgmental, and to choose kind, uplifting acts when interacting with others.

"Even if it's done quietly, inside your own mind," she told the residents often at House Meetings, "send out positive thought waves like seeds of loving compassion. The ripple effect of our combined, elevated thinking will change the stuck ways of our world much more than what social and political activists ever can do."

The circle of life. We experience it in cycles. Suffering and joy. Fear and Love. Perhaps we'll find the turmoil of such opposing energies encoded in humankind's DNA one day. It certainly seems we have good and bad, toxic and nurturing, in equal portions. I for one, know I would never have arrived at the satisfying life I have now, without having been to my own private hell first.

With each painful episode of *bad* comes a lesson that brings us closer to truly understanding *good*. We are continually being tested. Storms never stop coming. One day, sooner than later, I hope, nothing will be able to alter that sweet inner garden I know we're cultivating.

The altar of our spirit is within.

We learn to trust our inner Self by exploring this adventure we're having, right here, right now; and trusting there are infinitely more exciting ones to come, at exactly the right time.

So remember, those of you still suffering: All lessons of hardship count.

The how of embracing your *'I'* … is to just … *let it be.*

about the author

teZa Lord has chronicled her personal journey of transformation for decades with art and words. Now her work includes publishing nonfiction books that depict the sacred in the ordinary. Beginning as a student of expanded perception, her passions have centered on studying the evolution of human consciousness.

After completing her studies she exhibited and taught precious metals body-art. Then her images documented relationships between people and the natural world. Through botanical illustration, specializing in South American plant research (in affiliation with Harvard University), then painting and sculpting mixed-media compositions, her exhibited work was called "visionary" and her, "a naturalist."

Years of world adventure as an itinerant artist followed, including stints in film production in the US and the Caribbean; inter-island shipping from Dominica; a restaurant in the Virgin Islands; a jeweler, studio painter and sculptor in Israel and England. Back in the States, Lord was a furniture maker in New York City; a garden designer using living materials, stone, and water in East Hampton and Sarasota.

After marrying, Lord nurtured a blended family with her husband. During that era Lord switched from gallery-exhibiting object-art to being a storytelling-author who arts. Currently, along with publishing, she hosts yoga, chanting and meditation gatherings, and, as a spiritual activist, speaks about compassionate consciousness whenever asked.

Along with her years-long spiritual blog Lordflea.com, teZa's true life adventures are available as illustrated books. Her nonfiction narratives include:

"In the 'I' ... Easing Through Life-Storms"
"Zen Love ... The True Journey of a Blended Family"
"Hybrid Vigor ... a True Reveal of Love"

Join teZa's contributions to uplifting humankind's possibilities by planting positive *thought-seeds*, sharing positive thoughts. Sign up for her info-e's and receive her *free meditative audial clips* at tezalord.com. Or follow her Facebook, Twitter, Instagram offerings @tezalord. She'd love to hear from you! dearteza (at) gmail (dot) com

Lord's mantra is, "Love is the weapon of mass illumination."